D1572624

BASIC BOOK OF **CHRYSANTHEMUM GROWING**

IN THE SAME SERIES

Vegetable Growing
Flower Gardening
Rock Gardens and Pools
Rose Growing
Dahlia Growing

OTHER TITLES IN PREPARATION

BASIC BOOK OF CHRYSANTHEMUM GROWING

W. E. SHEWELL-COOPER
MBE, NDH, FLS, FRSL, Dip. Hort. (Wye), D Litt

SPECIALIST ADVISER
Jack Woolman

Managing Director, H. Woolman Ltd,
Chrysanthemum Specialists, and
Vice-Chairman of The National
Chrysanthemum Society

BARRIE & JENKINS
COMMUNICA - EUROPA

First published 1975
by Barrie & Jenkins Ltd,
24 Highbury Crescent, London N5 1RX

ISBN 0 214 20125 2

Photoset, printed and bound
in Great Britain by
REDWOOD BURN LIMITED
Trowbridge & Esher

Contents

List of illustrations

Black and white photographs and line drawings

Colour plates facing page

Acknowledgements
The author is most grateful to Mr Jack Woolman for supplying colour photographs. He would also like to thank Mr R. H. M. Robinson, of the Harry Smith Horticultural Photographic Collection, for kindly supplying the colour photographs facing pages 64, 97 and 128, and Mr Ernest L. Crowson, for all the black and white photographs.

to two of my grandchildren
Irene Marie Avril Shewell-Cooper
and
Caerveth Wray Shewell-Cooper

Preface

In 1964 we formed The Good Gardeners' Association, which advises amateurs all over the world on how to grow better fruit, flowers and vegetables by using organic methods, and rejecting purely chemical fertilizers. The Good Gardeners' bulletin can be read each month by those who are keen to follow up the latest methods. Please write to me for more details of this Association.

At the Arkley Manor Research Station, Arkley, near Barnet, experiments and demonstrations are always in progress. They show the great value of composting and minimum cultivation. Readers of this book, and especially Fellows of The Good Gardeners' Association, are very welcome to come and see the work being done.

I do hope you will like this *Basic Book of Chrysanthemum Growing*. At the back of the book is a complete glossary of terms which, if you are a beginner, you may like to study first.

This is the fourth book in the series of Basic Books of Gardening. Much of its substance was published originally in *The A.B.C. of Chrysanthemums*, now out of print, and I am delighted to have had the co-operation of Mr Jack Woolman, Vice-Chairman of The National Chrysanthemum Society, in the work of revision and updating. His expertise has been invaluable, and I cannot thank him enough for his help and advice.

Many other people have helped me with the preparation of this book. I should like to pay tribute to the late 'Bert' Shaw, my right-hand man in the gardens of the Cheshire Agricultural College during the thirties, and also to George Atkins, that excellent grower who worked on my staff at the Swanley Horticultural College. These were men of the soil who knew how to grow plants and who first encouraged my enthusiasm. So particular thanks are due to them.

Mrs Gweneth Johnson, Dip.Hort.(Swanley), who was on my staff for many years, both during the war and afterwards, has corrected the proofs, for which I am most grateful.

Thanks must also go to Mrs Toni Hartland and Mrs Helen Belfante for typing the manuscript so assiduously.

W. E. SHEWELL-COOPER

May 1975

Arkley Manor,
Arkley,
South Herts.

1 The History of the Chrysanthemum

One can hardly deal with the history of the chrysanthemum without mentioning right at the beginning the wonderful work done by The National Chrysanthemum Society during the past 124 years. This Society had, as its first headquarters, The Amherst Arms, Shacklewell Lane, Hackney, but later they were transferred to the Manor Rooms, Stoke Newington. In the early days the Society seems to have catered for the inner man, because some seventy exhibitors or so sat down each year to a gargantuan dinner where there was much eating and drinking.

In 1883, the Chrysanthemum Society changed its name from The Borough of Hackney Chrysanthemum Society to The National Chrysanthemum Society, and by 1890 there were seventy-five affiliated societies taking a great interest in this lovely flower. By 1897 the number of societies had grown to 135, and today stands at 1400.

Experts who are good at figures assure me that currently there must be over 8500 acres devoted to the cultivation of chrysanthemums, and it is said that the value of the flowers sold in the market, grown under glass, is in the region of £24,000. It is a flower that has world-wide popularity and I have met keen chrysanthemum growers not only in Europe and Japan, but also in Canada, South Africa and Australia.

It is very difficult to discover whether the chrysanthemum was really first known in Japan or in China. Both countries claim the flower as theirs. The earliest recorded statements, however, are those of Confucius in the year 500 B.C. The chrysanthemum is still regarded by some people as an Eastern flower, and so it is, and in those days long before the birth of Christ, the flower was certainly venerated if not actually worshipped. So highly was it prized that the Chinese made laws prohibiting the exportation of plants.

It seems, however, that some plants trickled into Korea and then on into Japan, for there is a record that they arrived there in

A.D. 386. So the Chinese had been able to keep them to themselves for some 800 years! The Chinese, it must be said, do not appear to have tried working on the plants in order to improve them; but the Japanese did do this, and so much so that the flower soon became the national emblem. In fact, just as the Queen may give the GCVO as a high personal honour to a citizen of Great Britain, so the Emperor of Japan gives the Grand Cross of the Order of the Chrysanthemum! It came to mean, therefore, far more to the Japanese than the rose to the English.

Although today one normally thinks of the chrysanthemum as a large round bloom, the ones that appeared in the chrysanthemum shows in Japan as long ago as A.D. 900 were small and incurved. They had long, wiry stems which were specially tied and trained by Japanese gardeners to form beautiful and unusual plants.

There has been some argument as to when the chrysanthemum first reached the shores of this country. It is recorded that a French captain, Louis Blanchard, brought a large-flowered specimen to Europe from China in 1789. This purple variety reached Kew Gardens in 1790. Earlier records, however, state that a much smaller-flowered kind of chrysanthemum reached England in 1764, but for some reason or other it disappeared within a few years.

It was probably an article in a botanical magazine in the late 1790s which caused gardeners to ask for further varieties. These were eventually imported from China and Japan, so that by 1826 some eighty-seven different varieties had been introduced. A French grower, Captain Bernet of Toulouse, produced chrysanthemum seeds in 1827 with the result that many new varieties were introduced. It wasn't long, however, before the English growers started to do the same thing. Mr Charles Wheeler produced the first English chrysanthemum seeds in his gardens at Oxford.

Robert Fortune helped by bringing in other chrysanthemum types like Pompons round about 1843, and by 1846 these were shown to the Royal Horticultural Society.

Although the National Chrysanthemum Society can trace back its history to 1846, it isn't really the oldest specialist society. The Norfolk Chrysanthemum Society can claim an earlier beginning in 1829. Birmingham had its first Chrysanthemum Society meeting in 1836, just at a time when a new large Incurved Chrysanthemum was raised in Jersey. Today Versailles is known for its famous Horticultural College, but in 1838 it was made famous by the huge Incurved Chrysanthemum, called The Queen of England, produced in John Salter's nursery. This was undoubtedly the beginning of the many glorious Incurved varieties seen at today's shows.

We must once again take off our hats to Robert Fortune, for in 1861 he sent home from China and Japan seven new types and varieties. These had petals which, instead of curving inwards in the normal way, hung outwards and downwards. By 1870, well over forty new varieties of the reflexed type were available to amateurs and cut-flower growers. Thus, by the centenary of the chrysanthemum's arrival at Kew, 1890, the flower had really become established in England.

The popularity of this queen of autumn flowers has never decreased. We can be thankful to several great experts who, during the last twenty years and more, have raised and introduced new varieties. I think, for instance, of that very well-known variety, Sweetheart, introduced by Johnson Bros., of Tibshelf. What should we have done without Harry Woolman of Shirley, who has introduced remarkable varieties like John Woolman, a large pink? H. Shoesmith of Woking was another great raiser of first-class varieties, like Victor Shoesmith and Fred Shoesmith. One cannot leave this list without also mentioning John Maher, who gave us Loveliness, and William Rootes, who produced Cranford Yellow.

It is now possible to grow chrysanthemums all the year round. One can have beautiful flowering pot plants no higher than a foot or so. There are singles and doubles, hardy types like the Koreans that may be left out of doors, and cascade types that should be encouraged and allowed to tumble down wire-netting provided at the base of the pot for the purpose. The chrysanthemum is probably the best cut flower grown today. The flowers last well, and can be sent from one part of the country to another without spoiling. Also, since the flowers and stems are rather heavy and bulky, we shall never get big imports from other countries.

Originally, the chrysanthemum may have been an Eastern flower, but it is now so naturalized that it is almost more British than the British.

2 The Official Classification

This classification of chrysanthemums, showing a few examples for each section, is as set out by The National Chrysanthemum Society, and is quoted with permission.

Late-flowering Chrysanthemums
Indoor varieties

Section 1 *LARGE EXHIBITION*
Shirley Primrose, Harry Gee, Mark Woolman

Section 2 *MEDIUM EXHIBITION*
Cossack, Birmingham

Section 3 *EXHIBITION INCURVED*
(a) *large-flowered*: Shirley Model, Woolman's Perfecta
(b) *medium-flowered*: Minstrel Boy, Vera Woolman

Section 4 *REFLEXED DECORATIVES*
(a) *large-flowered*: Elizabeth Woolman, Bridal Gown
(b) *medium-flowered*: Joy Hughes, Princess Anne

Section 5 *INTERMEDIATE DECORATIVES*
(a) *large-flowered*: Balcombe Perfection, Daily Mirror
(b) *medium-flowered*: Leslie Tandy, Woking Perfection

Section 6 *ANEMONES*
(a) *large-flowered*: Raymond Mounsey, Marion Stacey
(b) *medium-flowered*: Red Rolinda, Thora

Section 7 *SINGLES*
(a) *large-flowered*: Peggy Stevens, Red Woolman's Glory

(*b*) *medium-flowered*: Chesswood Beauty, Edwin Painter

Section 8 POMPONS
Mademoiselle Elise Dorcan, Golden Climax

Section 9 SPRAYS
Aphrodite, Exmouth Pink

Section 10 SPIDERY *etc.*
Green Nightingale, Rayonnante

Section 11 ANY OTHER TYPES

October-flowering Chrysanthemums Cultivars in Sections 13, 14, 15 and 16 are eligible for exhibition at both Early-flowering and Late-flowering Shows, as follows:

Section 13 (a) and (b)   in Sections 3 and 23 (a) and (b)
Section 14 (a) and (b)   in Sections 4 and 24 (a) and (b)
Section 15 (a) and (b)   in Sections 5 and 25 (a) and (b)
Section 16   where a class is provided

Section 13 INCURVED DECORATIVES
(*a*) *large-flowered*: True Form, Cheddar
(*b*) *medium-flowered*: Goldkist

Section 14 REFLEXED DECORATIVES
(*a*) *large-flowered*: White May
(*b*) *medium-flowered*: Jennifer Squires

Section 15 INTERMEDIATE DECORATIVES
(*a*) *large-flowered*: Golden Galleon, Susan Alesworth
(*b*) *medium-flowered*: James Bond

Section 16 LARGE OCTOBER-FLOWERING
Fantastic

Section 17 SINGLES

Section 18 POMPONS

Section 19 SPRAYS

Early-flowering Chrysanthemums Outdoor varieties

Definition of an Early-flowering Chrysanthemum: 'An Early-flowering Chrysanthemum is a cultivar which blooms in a normal season in the open ground before 1 October without any protection whatsoever.' This definition does not debar exhibitors from protecting blooms from weather damage. (See Rule 3 of *Rules for Judging*)

Section 23 INCURVED DECORATIVES
    (a) *large-flowered*: Ermine, David Shoesmith
    (b) *medium-flowered*: Martin Riley, Yellow Nugget

Section 24 REFLEXED DECORATIVES
    (a) *large-flowered*: Grace Riley, Shirley Sensation
    (b) *medium-flowered*: Early Red Cloak, Eve Gray

Section 25 INTERMEDIATE DECORATIVES
    (a) *large-flowered*: Evelyn Bush, Rosedew
    (b) *medium-flowered*: Cricket, Bill Else

Section 26 ANEMONES
Premier

Section 27 SINGLES
Margaret Rose, Kitty

Section 28 POMPONS
Cameo, Fairie

Section 29 SPRAYS
Lilian Hoek, Golden Orfe

Section 30 ANY OTHER TYPES

3 Raising Chrysanthemum Plants

The usual way of raising chrysanthemum plants is by means of cuttings. Early-flowering varieties are planted outside and Late-flowering varieties are potted up. At the end of the year, from each plant it should be possible to produce five or six more of the same variety. An increasing number of new plants can be raised each season from these.

Like everything else, however, there are difficulties to be overcome – pests to combat and diseases to prevent. Furthermore, as with all vegetative propagation, there is a tendency to deterioration. It is therefore most important to take considerable care in the selection of plants for propagation. Suggestions will be made throughout the book as to how these things may be done. The great importance of selecting healthy plants cannot be over-emphasized.

Seed Sowing
Plants raised from seed are always more vigorous. The great disadvantage of seed sowing, however, is that one cannot guarantee that the plants produced will be true to type or variety. When taking cuttings, vegetative propagation as it is called, the plants produced are exactly the same in every detail as their parent.

It is possible, however, to buy the seeds of perennial chrysanthemums. (Please note here that I am not referring to the annual chrysanthemum at all.) These seeds come from Japan but are available from British seedsmen, and can be had in (a) an Early-flowering mixture and (b) a Late-flowering mixture. A packet of twenty-five seeds (1975) costs twenty-five pence. In the case of the Early-flowering mixture, one invariably gets many plants with double flowers, some with semi-double flowers and others bearing single open blooms. The colours of the flowers may cover the whole range: white, pink, bronze, yellow and almost red.

In the first year from seed, the flowers produced are usually about 3 in. in diameter and the stems may be no more than 2 ft in height. From these plants it is possible to increase the stock by means of cuttings taken early the following season, with the result that from the new plants flowers can be obtained 4 in. or more across, on stems of 3 ft to 3 ft 6 in.

By raising plants in this way, it is possible to select the best colours and types and to propagate from them. There are always seedlings that are not particularly beautiful: these may be discarded. With the Late Mikado mixture, curiously enough, it is possible to get an even wider colour range and type range than with the Early-flowering mixture. I have known there to be large Incurveds and medium Pompons as well as Anemone-flowered and Spider-flowered varieties. It is possible, therefore, to gamble on producing a new and valuable variety which could, of course, be named after one's wife or girl friend!

Having bought the packets of seeds, say, in January, there is plenty of time to prepare the boxes and buy the seed compost for the seed sowing. Standard seed trays, 14 in. long by 8½ in. wide and 2½ in. deep, can be bought already made up or in pieces cut to the right size for making up by the keen 'do-it-yourself' gardener. The moment the boxes are made up they should be dipped in Rentokil preserving liquid, so that they last a number of years. (Plastic seed trays are also available.)

Seed trays that have been used in previous years must be thoroughly cleaned with a dry scrubbing brush. They should then be dipped in a 2½ per cent solution of formaldehyde for at least half an hour in order to eliminate any diseases that may be present. After the dipping, the boxes should be put out to dry, preferably in the open. Be careful when using formaldehyde because the fumes can be most unpleasant, and for young people could be dangerous. Some people have actually done the work wearing Second World War gas masks!

To save making up a complicated compost, Alex No-Soil Compost should be bought ready for use. When it comes from the suppliers it will be fairly dry. To make certain that it is sufficiently moist, tip however much is to be used into a bucket or zinc bath containing some water. It can then be turned and stirred to make it moist. There should not be any excess water. This does make sure that the compost is moist enough to give good germination of the seed. Place this compost in the seed boxes, which should have the necessary slits at the base for drainage. (When the bases of the boxes are made up, the lengths of wood should be nailed on so that there are spaces in between.)

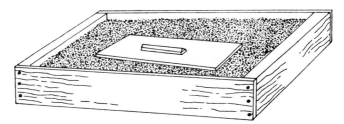

Firming down the compost in the box with a wooden presser

Press the compost down in the trays with a flat wooden presser, and see that the compost is just as firm around the edges and corners as in the centre. When level and equally firm right the way through, there should be a space of ½ in. from the top of the levelled compost to the top of the box.

It is on to this levelled compost that the chrysanthemum seeds will be sown. It pays to space the seeds out about 2 in. apart, and as they are not easy to see, they may be treated with a little lime first to turn them white. Press the seeds into the compost ⅛ in. down with the point of a pencil and then sieve a little more of the compost over the top to cover. Special fine mesh sieves may be bought from the ironmonger for the purpose. Alternatively, the 'do-it-yourself' gardener may make his own sieve by fixing a piece of perforated zinc on to a bottomless seed tray.

Use the presser for firming the compost over the seeds – a light pressing is quite sufficient. Now place over the box a sheet of glass and a piece of brown paper and stand the box on the staging of the greenhouse, keeping the temperature at about 60 degrees F. Every morning the glass should be removed and turned over so that the moisture which will have accumulated on the under side can dry off.

The moment the seedlings appear the glass should be removed. The brown paper, however, should be left on for three more days. It helps, after this, to keep the atmosphere of the house slightly damp and so the pathways and walls may be syringed over with clean water once a day.

If, at sowing time (which is usually in March), there should be a dull, cool period, it may be advisable not to water the boxes of seedlings at all. The chrysanthemum seedlings should not, of course, be under- or over-watered; it is never advisable to apply water if the compost is sufficiently moist, as the plants do not really need it. When the weather is warm and the house dry the leaves transpire a lot of moisture, and it is then that the roots need to take in more water.

Allow the seedlings to go on growing in the boxes until they are about 2 in. high and then pot them up individually into 3-in. plastic pots, once again using No-Soil Compost plus the special plant foods that are supplied with it. If the pots have been used before, they should be well washed in moderately hot water and then laid out in the sunshine to dry. With the special plastic pots there is no need to put any crocks in the bottom, because the drainage holes are well distributed and the base of the pot slightly raised.

Hold the seedling by its leaves in the centre of the pot with one hand, using the other hand to fill up the pot with the compost. When the pot is quite full and the roots are covered, firm the soil around the plant, applying the pressure to the soil just inside the rim of the pot and tapping it lightly on the bench at the time. If you do not think the pot is full enough, add a little more compost, firm and tap again until the compost is level to within $\frac{1}{4}$ in. of the top of the pot. It is necessary to leave this amount of room to allow for watering.

Now put the chrysanthemum seedling in its pot on the staging of the greenhouse and give it a good watering through the fine rose of a can. Try to keep the temperature of the house at about 55 to 60 degrees F at night; you can always allow it to rise to 65 to 70 degrees F during the day on account of extra heat from the sun. When the plants start growing, try and get them on to some shelving, even if this is put up temporarily, so that they are nearer the glass; this stops them from becoming long and lanky.

It should be possible to get the plants out of the greenhouse by the end of the first week of April and to put them temporarily into frames or under cloches where they can be hardened off. The idea is to get them used to outdoor conditions gradually. This should mean that by the third week of April or early May the chrysanthemums can be planted out in the open where they are to grow. Those who live in the colder parts of the north and are frightened that the chrysanthemums may be cut down by a late frost had better not plant out in the open until, say, the middle of May.

As for the preparation of the ground and the care of these chrysanthemums out of doors, reference must be made to Chapter 6. In the case of plants raised from the Late Mikado mixture, however, plants in 3-in. pots will have to be potted up into 6-in. pots and later into larger pots still. The advice given in Chapter 8 applies.

Division

It is possible, although seldom practised, to increase the number of chrysanthemum plants by what is called division. This is invariably done in the case of outdoor varieties and with hardy kinds. Readers who do not have a greenhouse, therefore, and who cannot afford or have no wish to erect one, may leave the plants growing out in the open, and divide them in the spring just as growth starts.

There are difficulties, of course, and especially in the north because not all varieties of chrysanthemum are completely hardy. So it is important to protect the old plants in November by covering them with glass cloches. When March comes, or maybe mid-April in the north, the plants may be forked or dug up carefully. When they are on the surface of the ground, they can be split into two, three or four parts by plunging hand-forks back to back into the centre of the clumps and then easing the handles apart. The old stem or stems and centre roots should, of course, be discarded and the outside range of roots, with their new shoots growing up, planted out where they are to grow.

The Stools or Stock Plants

When a chrysanthemum plant has flowered and the main growth of the season is over, the leaves having turned yellow, the stems may be cut down to within, say, 12 in. of soil level. In January or February the stems could be cut down still further, to 3 in. This, the old stem, the roots below and any young growths that may be growing up from the roots at the base of the stem, is what the gardener calls the stool.

An old stool with shoots growing up from the base

It is from the stool that cuttings are taken, and because it is going to be the parent of a number of new plants it is very important to take care in its selection. Never, under any circumstances, keep the stools of plants which have been badly affected by disease in the summer or autumn. This is especially true in the case of such a serious trouble as the Aspermy virus. The gardener must watch his plants while they are growing, and if the flowers appear twisted or ragged, or if the petals are peculiarly coloured, then virus must be suspected. Discard plants that have been badly attacked by eelworm and any that have shown signs of serious wilt diseases. It is far better to be safe than sorry.

Be careful, therefore, each season to choose only the best stools for propagation purposes. It is undoubtedly the man who is ruthless about getting rid of 'suspicious' plants who gradually builds up a healthy vigorous stock year after year.

At the end of October or early November the stools should be dug up carefully and most of the soil shaken off the roots or removed by hand. In the case of varieties where cuttings will not be needed until the end of February or early March, any young growths developing from the base of the plants must be cut off almost to their base. In years when little black slugs have proved a great nuisance it may well be worth washing the roots under a running tap, so as to remove the soil completely.

It is convenient to obtain standardized boxes about 18 in. long, 12 in. wide and 3–4 in. deep, and to put coarse sedge peat into the bottom of these boxes 1 in. deep. The stools should then be placed upright in the boxes as close to one another as convenient, and when they are sitting upright and firmly in position, a 1-in. layer of sedge peat should be put over the top, and given a light watering. Great care should be taken to see that the varieties are properly labelled. This can be done either by tying a small wooden label to the stem of each stool, or by laying lengths of bamboo, cut to fit the width of the box, between rows of different varieties, and then clearly labelling the ends of the rows.

Another method of storing the stools is to bring them into the greenhouse after the bulk of the soil has been shaken or brushed off. The stools are then planted upright, no deeper than $\frac{1}{2}$ in. or so, as close together as possible in beds 3 or 4 ft wide. Paths 2 ft wide should be allowed in between the beds so that the gardener can get among the plants. When the stools are in position they should be covered with a 1-in. layer of medium grade sedge peat which should be given a light watering afterwards. Once again, take care over labelling the stools clearly, allowing a 1-ft space between each variety.

From time to time the stools in their beds should be given a light syringing with water in order to encourage the production of cuttings. The soil, however, should never be allowed to become sodden and the temperature of the house should never be higher than 40 degrees F for the first three weeks at least. At the end of a month, the temperature may be allowed to rise to 50 degrees F. Chrysanthemum stools must be allowed to have their winter rest.

In the case of the winter-flowering varieties that are grown in pots, there is really no need to disturb the plants at all, once the stems have been cut down to within 2 ft of soil level. Then a second cutting down to within 6 in. can be done two months later. In fact, if there is plenty of room, the pots that are to be retained may be kept in the greenhouse or in a deep frame where there is plenty of air and light. The pots should not need watering for a number of weeks, and the temperature should not be more than 40 degrees F during that period.

Never coddle the stools, but protect them against serious frost and stop them from being 'drowned' by too much rain. They will be very happy in a frame or a cold greenhouse, especially one like a Dutch Light greenhouse where there is, of course, plenty of light. The boxes containing the stools will also go happily into a frame. The glass light of the frame can be well ventilated, except when the temperature drops below freezing point or when the rain tends to beat in. During extreme frosty periods, it is necessary to cover the glass of the frame with sacking, especially in the north.

In January the boxes can be moved into the greenhouse. During the first week the temperature may rise to 45 degrees F and during the second week and onwards, to 50 degrees F. Stand the boxes on the staging of the greenhouse, which should first be covered with fine cinders or small gravel to help prevent excessive loss of moisture.

Stools and Warm Water Treatment

Because the minute eelworms, which cannot be seen with the naked eye, cause infinite trouble to plants (see Chapter 17), it is a good plan to ensure the production of eelworm-free cuttings by adopting the warm water treatment. The basic method is to put the stools into warm water at a temperature of 115 degrees F for five minutes.

Propagation Times

The stools of varieties that need to be started into early cutting production may be brought into the greenhouse in November. In the case of varieties to be grown for exhibition, the stools usually come in about Christmas time, as do the Late-flowering Singles, the Pompons and the Decoratives. The varieties that are normally rooted in March may be left out in the cold frames until the beginning of February; this makes it important, as will be seen, to keep the various varieties and types separate in different boxes.

As has already been said, the temperature from now on is increased to 50 degrees F. This means that it is possible to give more water and so promote rapid growth.

When to Take Cuttings

Large specimen varieties	November
Large exhibition kinds	December and January
Exhibition show kinds	January and early February
Late-flowering Singles, Pompons	late January and February
Early-flowering outdoor kinds	mid-February and March
Dwarf Decorative plants	April and early May

Preparing and Striking the Cuttings

When the time comes for selecting and taking the cuttings, there should be a number of shoots, about 4 or $4\frac{1}{2}$ in. long, growing around the base of the stool. These should be stout, strong and fresh, for shoots that have been allowed to remain on the stool all through the winter produce cuttings which, when struck, seldom root well. That is the reason why it is advisable, when boxing the stools in the winter, to cut back any growths there may be, right to the base.

Gardeners often get strong new cuttings actively produced by raising the temperature of the greenhouse to about 60 degrees F for ten days when cuttings are needed, and then dropping the temperature down to 50 degrees F once plenty of shoots are seen to be growing. Another method is to have thin electric plastic-covered heating cables, hidden in the gravel or ashes on the staging. The electricity provides bottom heat. The local Electricity Board official will be glad to provide full information on this subject without charge.

If the reader has no greenhouse, it is possible to run a small soil-heating cable in a frame and to switch on, say, in mid-February, so as to start the stools into active growth. The cuttings that are taken from the stools can then be struck in boxes or pots in the same frame.

While the stools are producing growths, either in the greenhouse or in the frame, it is often advisable to spray with liquid derris in order to keep down aphids.

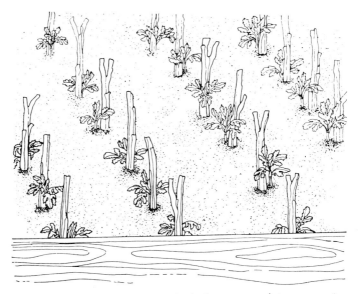

The old stools which have been out in the frames over winter are now producing shoots to be made into cuttings

The best cuttings come from the base of the shoots growing up from the stools, but in cases where there are not enough of these it is possible to make cuttings from the growths developing on the old stem. The disadvantage of taking stem cuttings is that they are apt to produce flowering buds very early, making it difficult to follow the normal stopping times (see pages 52–3). Ideally cuttings are made from moderately thick shoots about 3 in. long. Never select cuttings which have hollow stems or which look limp on the plants. Very thick shoots when made into cuttings take a long time to root and may actually split at the bottom.

Because the shoot develops from the roots of the plant, the stem is white at the bottom and green at the top. It is better not to retain any of the white portion. Using a very sharp knife or better still a razor blade, make a cut just below a node. This is sometimes called the joint and is the slightly swollen portion of the stem on which the leaves are grown. After this cut, the cut-

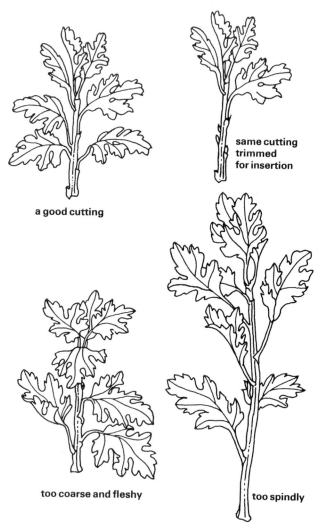

same cutting trimmed for insertion

a good cutting

too coarse and fleshy　　　**too spindly**

Choosing cuttings

ting should now be about 1½ or 2 in. long. If you are not used to raising plants in this way, you will find it useful to dip the base of the cuttings immediately into a Seradix hormone dust, which encourages roots to grow.

A hole about ½ in. deep should then be made, with a pencil or small dibber, in the compost in which this cutting is to root; the base of the cutting is put into position and firmed with two fingers of one hand. Some people strike their cuttings in standard-sized seed boxes 14 in. long, 8 in. wide and 2½ in. deep. In

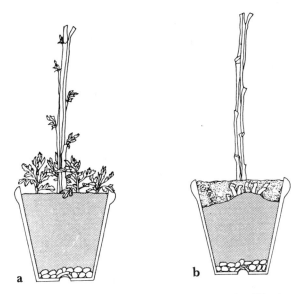

A stool from which cuttings can be taken (a) before (b) after

such a box it is possible to have six rows of cuttings – four to a row. After the cuttings are in position, the compost should be given a good watering through the fine rose of a can. Old-time gardeners much preferred to insert the cuttings around the edge of 3- or 3½-in. pots, putting in three or four cuttings to a pot. The disadvantage of using pots is that they dry out quickly, but on the other hand they warm up better and so the rooting of the cutting is, on the whole, quicker.

The material into which the cuttings are dibbled may be either Alex No-Soil Compost or a mixture of coarse silver sand and medium-grade sedge peat in the proportion of three to one. Recent experiments at Arkley have shown that a mixture of half fine soil and half Levington Compost is good. It is important that the sand or compost should be really coarse. Levington Compost needs watering far more than the preferred Alex No-Soil Compost which remains moist longer.

Having put the compost into the boxes or pots, and pressed it down lightly until level, it is quite a good idea to put on top of the compost an ⅛-in. layer of coarse silver sand. Thus, when the dibbled hole is made, some of the sand is taken down to the bottom of the hole and it is on this that the base of the cutting rests. This does encourage quicker and better rooting.

It will not be possible, of course, to take all the cuttings on the same day. It is necessary to watch the stools carefully for per-

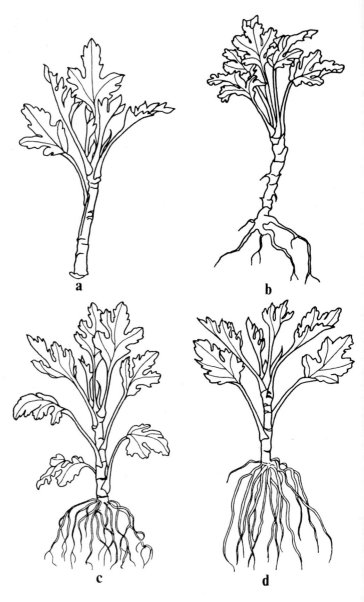

a. *A cutting cut just below a node*
b. *The first roots growing out*
c. *Plant ready for potting*
d. *Fully rooted cutting*

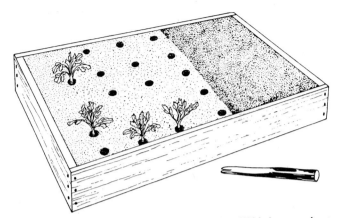

Seed box with the compost in and the cuttings being dibbled out evenly apart

haps three or four days and then cut off the shoots to the right length when they are ready. The moment the cuttings are in position in their boxes or pots, they must be placed on the staging of the greenhouse where the temperature can be kept at 60 degrees F at night, and where the actual temperature of the compost is in the region of 65 degrees F. The way to achieve this is to put on to the staging a largish bottomless box in which a 2-in. depth of medium-grade damped sedge peat may be placed. The top of the box should be covered with a sheet of glass.

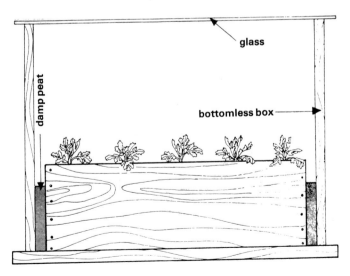

Bottomless box on the greenhouse staging

This is really a simple form of indoor propagating frame. It ensures a little extra heat where it is needed. Every morning the glass is removed and replaced upside down. If it should be extremely hot during the day, the glass may be lifted $\frac{1}{2}$ in. on one side to provide some ventilation. It must always be closed down, however, at night. (There are also some plastic propagators on the market which have proved most useful.)

By adopting this method it should be possible to ensure that the chrysanthemum cuttings are well rooted by the end of a fortnight (though I have known some varieties to delay rooting for three weeks). During the first few days that the cuttings are in this temporary frame it is often advisable to put a piece of brown paper over the glass, to provide a little shade.

The moment the cuttings have rooted they must be taken out of the propagator and put on to the staging of the greenhouse, where it will obviously be cooler. There they may remain for a fortnight or so before being placed in frames for hardening off. Care must always be taken, however, in this move to a cold frame if the cuttings are taken early. Generally speaking, it is necessary to wait until the middle of March before moving boxes or pots of cuttings from a warm greenhouse into a frame.

From now on the treatment varies somewhat, depending on whether the plant is an Early-flowering variety or not. With the Lates that are to be grown in large pots, the well-rooted young plants should be potted up into their plastic $3\frac{1}{2}$ in. pots. The Earlies, on the other hand, may be planted out into temporary frames and covered with Dutch Lights. These frames will have in the bottom of them a 2-in. layer of Alex No-Soil Compost plus the fertilizer base, used in accordance with the instructions on the plastic container. The alternative is to use a similar layer of John Innes Potting Compost 2.

Into either of these composts, the well-rooted young plants are spaced out with 4 in. between plants, the planting being done as firmly as possible. If the gardener sees to it that the soil below the compost is really hard, the cuttings root well into the compost and when they are taken out there is a minimum of damage to the roots. In fact, when the job has been done properly, there should be hardly any compost left in the frames when the chrysanthemums are taken up for planting outside in the places where they are to flower.

Readers who are going in for Early-flowering chrysanthemums for show will do well to pot up the plants indi-

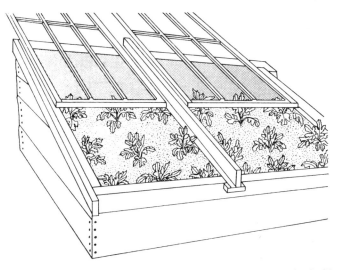

Frame being ventilated, with young chrysanthemum plants growing in No-Soil compost

vidually in 3½-in. pots as for the late varieties. Alex No-Soil Compost is put into the special plastic pots (which need no crocks) until they are half full. To make certain that the compost is firm enough, the base of the pot should be tapped lightly on a table or bench. The well-rooted young plant is placed in the centre of each pot and more of the compost poured in around the plant. The pot should then be tapped again to settle the compost evenly. Press the compost down with two fingers until its level is ½ in. below the rim of the pot.

The young plants in their pots (whether they be Early- or Late-flowering kinds) should go out into frames where they can be given some protection from frosts and excess rain until they are either potted on into large pots or, in the case of Early kinds, until they are planted out in the open. In the frames they should be sprayed overhead with water at about ten o'clock each day and they may need a good watering in addition after ten days. It is important to give the plants plenty of air as well as keeping them cool, for it is only in this way that they will be strong and sturdy. In fact, by the end of April in the south and on about 12 May in the north it should be possible to remove the lights altogether.

It may be said that chrysanthemums, on the whole, are fairly hardy, and that plants that have been hardened off as described are not likely to be completely killed by late spring frosts. There is always the danger, however, that a hard frost may damage the growing points of the plants, especially if it has proved necessary to 'stop' or 'time' the plant in the frame. (This means the pinching out of the growing points.) The result is that young growths will develop from the top buds that are left, and these growths will be soft and so susceptible to frost damage.

Irishman's Cuttings

Those who have not got a greenhouse and have perhaps only one small frame can, if they wish, delay the taking of cuttings until April in the case of outdoor varieties. The earlier cuttings should be cut back to their base so that off-shoots are encouraged. These can later be detached from the stools with their roots.

Shirley Crusader, a
Reflexed garden variety

4 No-soil Composts, John Innes Composts and Feeding

Unfortunately the word 'compost' is used by gardeners to indicate two entirely different types of organic substance. When vegetable refuse, straw and other organic matter is rotted down with an activator like fish manure in the special bin provided for the purpose, compost is produced. The soil mixture or other material used for striking cuttings or for pot plants is also called compost.

The whole question of composts for pot plants was revolutionized by the work of the John Innes Horticultural Institute in 1946. In the thirties a gardener had to remember how to make up fifty or so different composts which, it was said, had to be used to suit different types of plants. Today we know that there is no need for this and it is quite sufficient either to take the trouble to get the perfect kind of loam, sterilize it and then make up a John Innes compost, or to save both time and labour by buying in Alex No-Soil Compost which is ready for use.

John Innes Composts
The rules for John Innes Composts are as follows:

1. The compost must be in the right physical condition, be free from harmful organisms, and provide an adequate, balanced food supply.
2. The compost should be partially sterilized by heating.
3. Fertilizers should be added in the right proportion.
4. The compost should contain special loam, sedge peat and sand in the right proportions.
5. The ingredients of the compost should be partially sterilized separately, and then be mixed before the fertilizers are added.
6. The strictest hygiene should be practised in all matters.

The two composts recommended are:

Some Incurved Exhibition varieties: (l. to r.) Mavis Shoesmith, Maylen, Yellow Maylen, Lillian Shoesmith, Shirley Model

John Innes Seed Compost
  Compost No. 1   2 parts medium loam
               1 part good sedge peat
               1 part coarse sand
Add to each bushel* of this mixture $1\frac{1}{2}$ oz superphosphate of lime (16 per cent phosphoric acid) and $\frac{3}{4}$ oz ground limestone or chalk.

John Innes Potting Compost
  Compost No. 2   7 parts medium loam
               3 parts good moss peat
               2 parts coarse sand
Add to each bushel of this mixture $1\frac{1}{2}$ oz hoof and horn meal, $\frac{1}{8}$ oz grist, $1\frac{1}{2}$ oz superphosphate of lime, $\frac{3}{4}$ oz sulphate of potash and $\frac{3}{4}$ oz ground limestone or chalk.

It should be pointed out that it is always better to sift the superphosphate and sulphate of potash through a $\frac{1}{4}$-in. sieve before making up the mixture, or before adding the fertilizers to the compost. Readers should not try to vary the proportions of the fertilizers on their own account; these should be strictly adhered to, and the amounts not merely approximated but carefully weighed.

The same rule applies when measuring the soil. A wheelbarrow of a known capacity should be used, or a biscuit tin, the main thing being to make certain that the quantities are correct.

The potting compost may be used for pricking off for the majority of plants.

It is not always necessary to sterilize the sand if it is known to be free from weeds or organic matter. If a really good sedge peat is used from the Alex Peat Company, there is no need to sterilize this either. The special loam, however, must be sterilized and to get the best results it should first be passed through a $\frac{1}{2}$-in. sieve.

When sterilizing, by electricity, heat or steam, the temperature of the soil must be measured with a thermometer, never guessed. When sterilizing is over the hot soil should be removed immediately and spread out to cool. If the sterilizing has been done by steam this will also allow the excess moisture to evaporate.

Do not store sterilized compost for more than two months. It is always necessary to practise the strictest hygiene under glass. Don't, therefore, be particular about the sterilized soil and then careless about hygiene in other directions.

* A bushel of soil exactly fills a box measuring 22 in. by 10 in. by 10 in.

1. Be sure that the silver sand used is of a coarse texture. If it is fine, it cakes and is useless. If it is red, it probably has iron in it and will set hard. Sea sand is too salty. River bed sand is best.
2. Be sure that the peat is a sedge peat, and that it has been previously treated, for example by the Alex Peat Company. It will then arrive free from pests, diseases and weed seeds.
3. Be sure that the right fertilizers are added to the compost in accordance with the instructions given.
4. Feed as necessary with diluted Marinure, or Farmura.
5. See that the quantities in the case of each John Innes mixture are correct. Use a standard measure, like a seed tray 18 in. long, 14 in. wide and 3 in. deep.

Two more John Innes Composts

It has been discovered that if chrysanthemums are to be grown in 5-in. pots it is better to use what is called John Innes Potting Compost 3. Exactly the same quantities of sterilized loam, sedge peat and coarse sand are used as for John Innes Potting Compost, but to every two bushels of this mixture add 9 oz hoof and horn meal, 9 oz superphosphate, 4½ oz sulphate of potash and 4½ oz ground chalk.

Where plants are to be grown in 8- or 9-in. pots, John Innes Compost 4 is advised, and this means adding the following to two bushels of John Innes Compost: 12 oz hoof and horn meal, 12 oz superphosphate, 6 oz sulphate of potash and 6 oz ground chalk.

Sterilizing the Loam

Soil should be sterilized at 180 degrees to 200 degrees F for fifteen minutes, and should then be cooled.

It is possible to buy electric soil sterilizers and the local headquarters of the Electricity Board will provide the necessary information. The apparatus, unfortunately, is expensive.

For sterilizing small quantities of soil the domestic clothes-washing copper may be used. Two gallons of water should be put into the bottom of the copper and a bucket, perforated all over with ⅛-in. holes, 3 in. apart, may be hung from a crossbar. The bucket is filled with the soil to be sterilized and the water is then boiled. If a cover is kept over the copper the steam should penetrate the soil completely by the end of forty minutes, and the sterilization will be completed.

No-Soil Composts

As the result of much research work, it has been found possible to produce a compost which contains no soil at all. This consists of a special type of sedge peat plus a particular grade of silver sand, and it comes to the amateur already mixed for using. Inside the bag of No-Soil Compost will be found a small plastic container with the special plant foods inside, which have to be added to the compost. Full instructions are given as to how much to use and how it should be incorporated. I was first introduced to No-Soil Composts in 1959 and tried them out at The Horticultural Training Centre at Thaxted, of which I was then Principal. After the move to Arkley the experimental work was continued and the information obtained is now given in detail.

No-Soil Seed and Potting Compost contains no loam or soil and is a specially processed peat product. It has been formulated to produce better results than a traditional loam compost. It has been designed and balanced to suit British weather conditions and to produce a natural type of root growth similar to that produced in a normal soil, so that plants may be transferred from a loam compost into a No-Soil Compost or vice versa with perfectly satisfactory results.

The compost is composed of a specially selected and processed sedge peat and specific fine sand blended with fertilizers and trace elements. The fact that the bulk of the compost contains highly organic sedge peat enables it to hold nutrients well when used as a potting compost. Therefore, it does not require feeding any earlier than a normal soil. Further, when liquid feeds are given, a fuller benefit is experienced in the extra growth produced.

Normal No-Soil Compost is actually several composts in one, in that the main bulk of the material is a seed compost containing a low but adequate level of nutrition. Also, this seed compost can be converted into potting compost, No. 1, 2 or 3 as required, by the addition, in various proportions, of potting base; a sachet of this is contained in each pack.

Preparation of No-Soil Compost for Use

Before using No-Soil Compost for the striking of cuttings or for the growing on of plants, the compost should be moistened up with water at the rate of 8 to 10 pints per bushel. This moistening up is very important as it conditions the peat to take water afterwards. The compost should be spread out and the water applied through a fine rose and should then be turned several times to mix together the dry and wet peat. If there is time to spare, it is a good plan to put the compost up into a loose heap and leave it for several hours, so that the moisture spreads naturally through the whole heap.

When making up one of the potting composts, the 'base' should be added before the water. This potting base should be thoroughly mixed into the compost and this may require at least five or six turns. The potting compost should then be given the normal 6 to 8 pints of water per bushel.

For the Striking of Cuttings

No-Soil Compost is very suitable for this purpose. Seed boxes should be filled evenly with conditioned compost, struck off level and very lightly firmed with a board to obtain a level surface. Firming should only be very light, just sufficient to make the surface level so that when water is applied, it will spread and soak in evenly through the box. The prepared cuttings should be inserted in the normal way.

It is in the application of water that the main difference between growing in soil and in a peat compost lies. This, however, presents no difficulty when it is appreciated that peat is capable of holding a very large amount of water, and is also well aerated. This means that Alex No-Soil Compost holds three times more moisture than a loam compost and will dry out much more slowly in dull weather, but because of its aeration, it will dry out slightly quicker in warm bright weather.

With cuttings being rooted under dull cool conditions, therefore, it is important to avoid over-watering. The best procedure to follow, after the insertion of the cuttings, is to stand the boxes in shallow water until the compost appears slightly moist on the surface. Boxes should then be drained and placed on the greenhouse bench – the chrysanthemums themselves being shaded by sheets of newspaper during bright spells. Subsequent watering should be carried out very gently with a fine rose spray and in this way the compost will keep open and dry out relatively quickly. A heavy drenching spray will only serve to pan down the compost, so that it remains too wet too long.

For the late striking of chrysanthemum cuttings from mother plants in May and June, No-Soil Compost will be found to give far better results than John Innes Compost. In this case No-Soil Compost is better able to keep the base of the cuttings cool and moist. No-Soil Compost should not be allowed to dry out and should be watered when it still feels slightly moist to the touch.

No-Soil Seed Compost contains a low level of nutrients which will be available to the cuttings immediately after formation of roots. If it is intended that the cuttings should remain for some time in the compost after rooting, or if it is thought likely that potting may be delayed, then it is advisable to root the cuttings in a No. 1 potting compost. A No. 1 potting compost is made up by adding 11 oz of the potting base supplied, i.e. one third of the potting base sachet, to one bushel of compost. Owing to the high 'buffering' action of the sedge peat used, this fertilizer level will not inhibit or harm the developing rootlets, but once these roots are formed the availability of nutrients will enable the plants to make immediate growth, so cutting out any possibility of a check.

Growing On
For the growing on of young chrysanthemum plants, No-Soil Compost 3 should be used in both 3-in. and 9-in. pot stages. In making up a No. 3 compost all the potting base supplied in the sachet, i.e. 33 oz, should be added to the bushel of compost and thoroughly mixed in. After this, No-Soil Potting Compost should be conditioned with water as suggested above.

In chrysanthemum culture, there is one major difference between the two composts. With John Innes Compost it is traditional to ram the compost, particularly in 9-in. pots. Quite the reverse is the case with a No-Soil Compost; plants should not be over-firmed.

With the first potting on into 3-in. or 3½-in. pots, no crocks are required, even in clay pots. The pots should be filled loosely with compost, smoothed off level and the young plants planted with the minimum of firming. The young plants should then be watered in the normal way. A young chrysanthemum plant, as any newly potted plant, should be encouraged to make root and search for moisture, therefore do not keep the compost over wet during the first week or two. At the same time, avoid drying out. The compost should be watered when it still feels moist. For the first two weeks, therefore, water very gently, and after several waterings, the compost will settle down naturally to its normal compactness and behave similarly to soil.

If the above instructions are followed, it will be found that there will be a good ½ in. of watering space left at the top of the pot after the compost has settled down. A good watering space is very necessary as No-Soil Compost will hold a lot of water and, therefore, sufficient water should be given at each watering to moisten all the compost in the pot. A $\frac{1}{2}$-in. watering space will be sufficient for this purpose.

With No-Soil Compost, plants in a 3-in. pot will eventually be larger than is normally possible in a John Innes Compost. When this stage is reached, therefore, it must be appreciated that the small 3-in. pot is supporting a large plant with a large leaf area evaporating water. Adequate water must be given. Just prior to potting on into 9-in. pots, the young plants in the 3-in. pots should be given a thoroughly good watering or preferably a good soak from below in order to moisten the ball of compost right through. When potting on, the larger 9-in. pots should be crocked and loosely filled with No-Soil Compost 3 which has already been conditioned with water.

Barely fill the pots with No-Soil Compost so that when the young plant with its ball of roots is planted into the 9-in. pot, the level of loose compost is slightly below the rim of the pot. The level will drop to about $1\frac{1}{2}$ in. from the top of the pot, providing adequate watering space for the compost. As mentioned before, the compost should not be over-firm, and the young plant should be watered in the normal way. Subsequent water will settle the compost naturally.

Feeding

No-Soil Compost can be sufficiently loaded with nutrients at the outset to reduce feeding to a minimum. Under normal conditions, the nutrients supply (provided Alex Compost is used) is more lasting than with most loam composts. In practice, therefore, it will often be found that feeding may be delayed longer than would normally be expected with John Innes Compost 3.

In some circumstances, under optimum light and temperature conditions, a very rapid initial growth of plants (produced in No-Soil Compost) may benefit from earlier feeding in order to maintain the advantage gained. In other words, while No-Soil Compost 3 will produce a very good growth, even better results can come with some liquid feeding. This is because No-Soil Compost is able to make very good use of liquid feeds on account of the high nutrient retention properties of the sedge peat used.

In addition to this, the buffering action of the sedge peat has the advantage of levelling out over-high concentrations of feed given in error, i.e. strengths of feed which, in a John Innes Compost, might be expected to cause root damage. Therefore, where extra quick growth is desired or a larger plant is supported in a comparatively small pot, plants may easily be 'forced' with feed in No-Soil Compost, provided light and temperature conditions are right.

Two distinct types of feed are required by chrysanthemums. Nitrogen is required in greater abundance up to the 'taking' of the bud, after which potash should predominate. During the development of the bud, the uptake of phosphate will increase. A complete high nitrogen feed should be applied first, then, after the bud has 'taken', a high potash complete fertilizer should be used.

Solid and liquid feeds may be given, but for pot work, liquid feeds are strongly recommended. The application of weak liquid feeds applied frequently is a much more natural way of feeding, and avoids the high fluctuations in the chemical levels of a compost following infrequent heavy applications of a solid feed.

Chrysanthemums growing in No-Soil Compost 3 in 3-in. pots will probably not require feeding before six weeks after planting but, as mentioned above, occasional early feeds will certainly give even better results. After potting on into 9-in. pots containing No-Soil Compost 3, the chrysanthemums may well not require regular feeding until after eight to ten weeks from potting on, but here again, occasional liquid feeds from the fourth week will prove an advantage.

Once the plants are growing in the ground or their pots, they will need feeding. It is convenient to use a liquid for this purpose, and especially one with an organic base. Maninure fills the bill and may be bought in containers ready for dilution. Detailed instructions will be found on the label as to how this liquid plant food should be used, and later on in the chapter more implicit instructions are supplied.

In dealing with the problem of feeding chrysanthemums, it must be made clear that the yellowing of the leaves (called 'chlorosis' by the expert gardener) may be due to things other than starvation. Plants in pots that are over-watered suffer badly because the fibrous roots will die. Then, of course, no plant foods can reach the leaves. The foliage may turn bright green and yellow if the pots are standing in a spot where there is little or no light. Plants that are pot-bound, i.e. trying to grow in much too small a pot, may have yellow leaves as, of course, will plants that have not been fed at all.

Although chrysanthemums need small quantities of lime, most soils contain sufficient. In fact, the gardener should never use lime unless it is discovered that the pH is 6 or less. (For details of this form of notation, please see the Glossary, page 145.) When there is too much lime the calcium may prevent the plants from taking in the amount of iron they need, thus causing what expert gardeners call lime-induced chlorosis.

In such circumstances the answer is to use Sequestrene Plus at the rate of 1oz per gallon of water. A pint of this should be given to each plant and the deficiency of iron will be made up within a week or ten days. Ask your local horticultural chemist for this Sequestrene and make certain, when you use it, to apply it to the soil and not to allow it to get on the leaves. As a matter of fact Sequestrene Plus adds not only iron but manganese and magnesium as well, both of which may be needed. You can't get chrysanthemums to take up the iron they need by applying iron sulphate, as advised by some authors, because this soon gets locked up by the lime.

Chrysanthemums, in the normal way, need nitrogen, phosphates and potash: the nitrogen to feed the leaves and to produce the growth, the phosphates to help the production of roots and to ripen the stems, and the potash to promote sturdy growth, strong wood and nice firm blooms. If the nitrogen is over-done, the plants will be soft; if the potash is over-done, the leaves are brittle and the stems so hard that they won't easily take in water when cut. One can see, therefore, the importance of using a balanced liquid fertilizer like Marinure or Farmura, and applying it carefully, as advised in this chapter.

Liquid Plant Foods

Marinure and Farmura are ideal liquid fertilizers for feeding chrysanthemums. They contain all the essential plant nutrients in correct proportions, together with trace elements.

Up to the 'taking' of the bud, a complete food high in nitrogen should be given. For this purpose a general type should be used, at 1 part of concentrate to 600 parts of water, i.e. $\frac{1}{4}$ pint in 20 gallons of water, or 1 large dessertspoonful in 8 gallons. Where only occasional liquid feeds are given, the concentration at each feed should be increased to 1 in 300, i.e. $\frac{1}{4}$ pint of concentrate to 10 gallons, or 1 large dessertspoonful to 4 gallons.

After 'taking' the flower bud and during the swelling of the bud, a high potash liquid feed should be given, and Marinure (high potash) or Farmura should be used. Autumn conditions will be prevailing at this stage and the water requirements will be much less than during the summer. Therefore, in order to apply sufficient liquid feed, the more concentrated level of 1 large dessertspoonful to 4 gallons should be given with every watering, or at any rate every alternate watering.

A Special Note by Mr Jack Woolman (see Preface)
I recommend half soil and half Levington Compost. I put a thin layer of sand on top of this, which makes it easier to poke holes in it. Plants in peat composts must never be allowed to get completely dry because of the difficulty of wetting the peat again. Such pots need feeding sooner after potting on than when soil mixtures are used. I advise the use of Woolman's Organic Fertilizer spread on top of the pot and watered in. A teaspoonful will do, commencing in the last week or two of the 5-in. stage in the frames and then continuing every week from about three weeks after potting until the end of September.

5 'Pinching', 'Stopping' and 'Timing'

A chrysanthemum plant, if it is left alone, will eventually produce a flower bud at the top of the stem. This checks the upward growth and causes two or three buds in the axils of the leaves nearest the top of the plant to break out into growth.

a. Young plant from rooted cutting. If left to grow naturally, this would continue growing taller until the 'break bud' was produced
b. Plant stopped by removal of tip of main stem
c. The first breaks of lateral growths developing from the leaf axils on the main stem

If the gardener wishes the plant to produce these branches earlier, he 'pinches' out the tip of the plant before this break bud (as it is called) has appeared. The plant is then said to have been 'stopped'. The date on which the pinching out is done will differ from one variety to another, and so the word 'timing' is sometimes used. The growing point of the plant is pinched or cut off on a certain date so that the buds will flower at a certain time.

43

It should be clearly understood that there is a very definite relation between the date when a cutting is rooted and the date when that plant is stopped. Root a cutting in the month of January and the plant will have to be stopped, say, on 1 May. Root a cutting of that same variety in late March or early April and the stopping date would be likely to be sometime in June. Later on in the chapter, where stopping dates are suggested, the date for taking the cuttings is also given.

It has already been said above that if a plant is left alone it produces a bud at the end of its single stem. Because the upward growth of the stem is stopped by this bud (the break bud), the top three or four tiny buds in the axils of the leaves break out into growth. This is why the first flowering bud is called the 'break bud'. As a result a plant has a main stem and three or four branches. When each of these branches produces in its turn a flower bud at the top, this is known as the crown bud, or to be more correct, the first crown bud. This first crown bud can be pinched out with the thumb and forefinger, so that further growth is produced for a period of time until yet another flower bud appears to check the growth. This flower bud is known as the second crown.

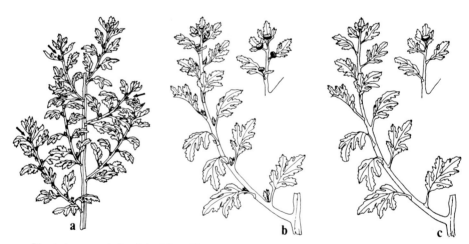

a. *Plant almost ready for disbudding. The centre bud developing at the end of each of the six breaks in the crown bud. The arrows indicate shoots that might be left in reserve until the first crown bud is seen to be developing satisfactorily*
b. *One break on the lateral growth before the bud has been secured*
c. *The break on the lateral growth as it should appear after securing the bud. All unwanted buds and all young shoots that were developing on the leaf axils have been removed*

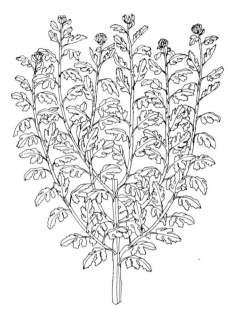

Plant fully disbudded. All young shoots have been removed from the leaf axils of the six lateral growths and six first crown buds have been secured

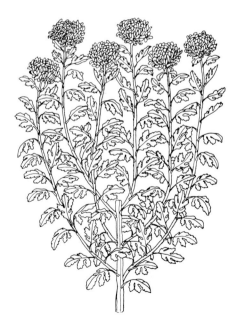

The same plant carrying six blooms from first crown buds

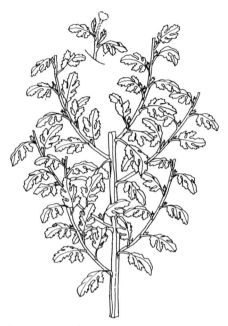

Plant stopped a second time by removal of the tip of each of the six first breaks. Young shoots called second breaks are appearing on the leaf axils. The inset shows the process of running on, and the rubbing out of the first crown bud. Many growers now prefer to remove also the young shoot immediately below the first crown bud and to allow the next lower shoot to run on to form a second crown bud

It is possible, yet again, to pinch out this bud and so ensure yet another set of laterals. The flower bud at the top of this final growth is known as the terminal bud.

The gardener who 'stops' or 'times' is deliberately preventing the plant from growing naturally and producing its flower buds and laterals when it feels inclined. He pinches out the top $\frac{1}{4}$ in. or so of the growth, so forcing the plant to produce its side growth earlier than it would naturally. It may be that he is anxious to produce some chrysanthemums for a particular date – a birthday, a christening, a flower show. If the variety were left alone it might flower much too early for the particular date in mind. On the other hand, grown naturally, the plant might flower too late. By adopting artificial means, the keen chrysanthemum grower is able to ensure, all being well, that the flowers will be ready when they are needed. It takes a lot of study coupled with a great deal of experience to know what to do with the various varieties under the particular conditions in which they are being grown.

Plant as it should appear a short time later. The centre bud developing at the end of each of the second breaks is the crown bud

Fortunately, there are chrysanthemum nurserymen whose delight is to specialize in this beautiful flower, and when they list the many differing varieties under their separate headings in the catalogues, they usually give some guidance on stopping and timing as well.

It could be said, of course, that the timing of chrysanthemums is more important in the case of indoor-flowering varieties than for those that are to grow in the open, but even with Early-flowering varieties, timing will help to ensure that the flowers are produced on a definite date. With the Earlies it is usual to stop while the plants are in the cold frames, before they are planted out in the open. If only the top $\frac{1}{4}$ in. is removed, uniform side growths are produced and these in their turn will carry, say, four good chrysanthemum blooms per plant. With Earlies, however, the weather can cause difficulties; when there is a lot of rain in the summer flowering tends to be late, and when there is a sunny droughty period flowering tends to be early.

Flowering times will also vary according to the variety of chrysanthemum. Further variations will be caused by location – a gardener in Westmorland will expect his chrysanthemums to flower much later than similar plants in a warm garden in

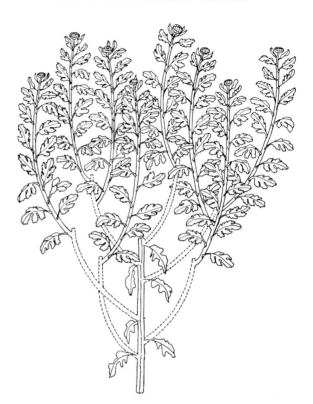

The second breaks fully disbudded. All young shoots have been removed from the leaf axils and eight second crown buds have been secured

Sussex, and by the type of soil – on the whole I have found that chrysanthemums flower a little later on heavy clay soils than on warm sandy loams.

The date recommended for stopping and timing determines the date when the cutting is to be struck. If, for instance, the catalogue or textbook says that a particular late variety needs stopping on 30 April, then the gardener knows that he must get the cutting struck in January. If he puts it off until February (the normal time), the young plant will not be sufficiently developed for the pinching out or stopping to be done effectively.

The interesting thing is that it is often necessary (with Earlies at any rate) to stop some plants of a particular variety, whereas others that have broken quite naturally may be left. Incidentally, the flowers and stems produced in the natural way always tend to be earlier than those produced by stopping on a similar date. The real worry – if it may be called that – about stopping

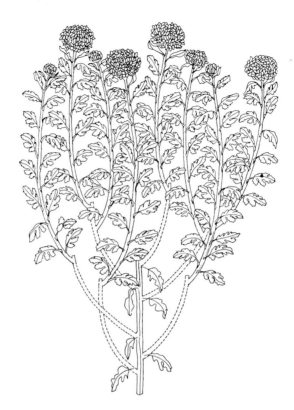

Plant coming into bloom on second crown buds

and timing is, of course, reserved for growers trying to produce flowers for exhibition at a particular show. The ordinary man in the street who just loves to grow chrysanthemums for the sake of their beauty, or because his wife loves plenty of cut flowers in the house, needn't be too worried about timing.

Keeping a Diary

Growers who are going to stop and time should undoubtedly keep a diary. It is only by carefully recording what has happened that the gardener can build up accurate information about his garden, its soil and its conditions. Gradually, therefore, he builds up a permanent record which will prove invaluable to him. This information will include the date the cutting was rooted, the date it was stopped, the date it produced its first crown buds, the date it flowered and so on. Weather conditions will also be noted, bearing in mind what has already been said about the effect of the weather on earliness and lateness.

Comparing Crown Buds

Readers who are wondering whether there is any difference between the flowers produced by the first crown buds and those produced by the second crown buds should know that, by and large, a bloom on a first crown bud of, say, an Exhibition variety, may easily carry four hundred more petals than a similar bloom produced on the second crown bud of that variety. In fact, there are unusual cases of gardeners who go on stopping their plants, with the result that the blooms produced by the terminal buds are almost single because they have so few petals on them!

Some varieties produce blooms with too many petals on the first crown buds, so that they are awkward and do not look perfect. The gardener, in this case, purposely takes his plant on to a second crown, and because this has fewer petals the bloom can compose itself perfectly. This can happen, in particular, with the large Exhibition varieties.

Colour and Stopping

It is worth recording that the colour of a particular variety may be improved by taking it on to a second crown bud. There are some wishy-washy pink varieties, for instance, where the colour becomes a lovely intense pink on the second crown bud. Definite yellows may turn out to be attractive bronze yellows at the second crown bud. It pays, therefore, to get catalogues from chrysanthemum specialists and to study carefully whether the plants should be grown on their first or second crown buds, and what stopping and timing may be necessary for each variety.

Stopping and Branches

It will be seen that when the main growth of the plant is pinched out, four good branches may be produced and any in excess of this may be pinched out while they are still small. These four side growths will then grow happily for about six weeks, after which they may be stopped again. As the result of this second stopping, three laterals may be allowed on the original four branches, thus giving twelve good stems per plant and, one hopes, twelve good chrysanthemums in consequence. This second stopping is often done in the case of mid-season varieties, the kinds that normally flower in late October and November.

One should not imagine, however, that varieties can be made to flower at any time by means of stopping methods. Some gardeners, for instance, have hoped to make late-October varieties flower in mid-December, but the very late stopping on two occasions has only resulted in flowers being produced late in the year that are not only poor in colour, but also terribly poor in texture, size and appearance.

Stopping Experiments

Readers who live in the north have particular difficulties with outdoor chrysanthemums because the autumn frosts are early. I have known good chrysanthemums growing outside in Lancashire, for example, to be ruined by frost on 25 September. A gardener who has no glass, therefore, aims to ensure that his plants flower early. He doesn't wait for the plants to break naturally but pinches out the growing points on a certain date and has plants in flower a fortnight or three weeks earlier.

The following chart is taken from one of the Official Trial Reports:

Name	Natural Break	Time of Flowering	Time of Stopping	Time of Flowering
Hurricane	12 June	27 September	31 May	10 September
September Glory	15 June	25 September	20 May	1 September
September Red	10 June	30 September	30 May	10 September

This table shows what can be done to bring about earlier flowering; growing points of the plant are pinched out three weeks before the natural breaking would take place. The buds of Early- and October-flowering cultivars do not normally need to be secured.

Helpful Tables for Stopping and Timing

It must be said quite clearly that no one can dare lay down any hard and fast rules for the perfect stopping dates of any variety. The stopping dates must take into consideration the weather, soil and local conditions. As has already been said, the stopping dates are also dependent on the date the cuttings are struck.

The tables given in the remainder of the chapter can therefore only act as guides. It is impossible to include the names of all varieties and especially so since novelties are being introduced year after year, and fashions change. The reader will be well advised to join The National Chrysanthemum Society which issues the *Chrysanthemum Manual* from time to time. This contains charts, under separate sections, giving the normal stopping dates advised for the best results.

LATE-FLOWERING CHRYSANTHEMUMS

Sections 1 and 2 LARGE and MEDIUM EXHIBITION

Name	Rooting Date	Natural Break or 1st Stop	2nd Stop	1st or 2nd Crown	Colour	Secure Bud
Bill Bye	mid-January	N.B.	—	1st	yellow	15 August
Cossack	mid-January	N.B.	N.B.	2nd	crimson	20 August
Gigantic	early January	1st week May	—	1st	chestnut	15 August
Mark Woolman	early January	2nd week April	—	1st	yellow	9 August
Shirley Primrose	early January	2nd week March	2nd week May	2nd	yellow	9 August

Section 3 EXHIBITION INCURVED

Name	Rooting Date	Natural Break or 1st Stop	2nd Stop	1st or 2nd Crown	Colour	Secure Bud
Shirley Crystal	early February	2nd week March	2nd week May	2nd	white	25 August
Shirley Model	end January	N.B.	—	1st	purple	15 August
Vera Woolman	early February	2nd week March	N.B.	2nd	yellow	25 August
Woolman's Royal	early February	1st week April	1st week June	2nd	purple	25 August
Yellow Maylen	early February	N.B.	N.B.	2nd	yellow	25 August

Sections 4 and 5 DECORATIVES

Name	Rooting Date	Natural Break or 1st Stop	2nd Stop	1st or 2nd Crown	Colour	Secure Bud
Balcombe Perfection	end January	N.B.	—	1st	bronze	1st week September
Bridal Gown	mid-February	1st week May	—	1st	white	1st week September
Elizabeth Burton	early February	N.B.	N.B.	2nd	pink	1st week September
Fred Shoesmith for November	mid-February	1st week June	—	1st	white	1st week September
Fred Shoesmith for Christmas	end February	1st week April	1st week June	2nd	white	1st week September
Princess Anne	end February	end March	N.B.	2nd	pink	1st week September
Shirley Sentinel	end February	1st week April	1st week June	2nd	bronze	1st week September
Snowshine	mid-February	2nd week April	N.B.	2nd	white	1st week September

OCTOBER-FLOWERING CHRYSANTHEMUMS

Section 13 INCURVED DECORATIVES

Name	Rooting Date	Natural Break or 1st Stop	2nd Stop	1st or 2nd Crown	Colour	Secure Bud
Crackshot	mid-February	mid-May	—	1st	pink	

Section 14 REFLEXED DECORATIVES

Name	Rooting Date	Natural Break or 1st Stop	2nd Stop	1st or 2nd Crown	Colour	Secure Bud
Firecracker	end February	early April	early June	2nd	red	
Jennifer Squires	end February	early April	early June	2nd	rose-pink	

Name	Rooting Date	Natural Break or 1st Stop	2nd Stop	1st or 2nd Crown	Colour
Section 15 INTERMEDIATE DECORATIVES					
Golden Galleon	end February	early April	early June	2nd	yellow
Goldplate	end February	mid-April	N.B.	2nd	gold
Susan Aylesworth	mid-March	N.B.	—	1st	pink
EARLY-FLOWERING CHRYSANTHEMUMS					
Section 23 INCURVED DECORATIVES					
Ermine	end February	N.B.	—	1st	white
David Shoesmith	early March	3rd week May	—	1st	bronze
Margaret Riley	end February	N.B.	—	1st	pink
Section 24 REFLEXED DECORATIVES					
Cloth of Gold	mid-March	N.B.	—	1st	yellow
Early Red Cloak	early March	N.B.	—	1st	crimson
Grace Riley	early March	3rd week May	—	1st	chestnut
Ruby Queen	early March	N.B.	—	1st	crimson
Shirley Sensation	end February	1st week May	—	1st	orange
Section 25 INTERMEDIATE DECORATIVES					
Evelyn Bush	early March	N.B.	—	1st	white
Keystone	early March	N.B.	—	1st	purple
Primrose Cricket	early March	N.B.	—	1st	yellow
Rockall	early March	N.B.	—	1st	pink
Shirley Victoria	end February	N.B.	—	1st	chestnut
Woolley Charm	early March	N.B.	—	1st	bronze
Woolley Jewel	early March	1st week May	—	1st	white

Securing the Bud

Reference has already been made earlier in the chapter to bud securing, but as the term appears in the charts it may be as well to refer to the matter again. Bud securing is really a question of disbudding and dis-shooting. One disbuds a rose, for instance, by pinching off the little flower buds at the side and near the top of a flowering shoot. This leaves the end bud to bloom alone. The result should be one really good rose per stem instead of a cluster of smaller blooms.

In the case of chrysanthemums, the terminal bud appears and the gardener wants to ensure that it develops properly. He thus carefully pinches out the little flower buds just below the terminal bud as well as any incipient lateral growths there may be. He removes all growths and buds that may compete with the main flower bud, and this is what is called securing the bud.

6 Earlies Out of Doors

No one who has a garden can be excused for not growing the Early-flowering chrysanthemum. First of all, it flowers well without a lot of trouble. Secondly, many varieties have long flowering periods. Thirdly, it is possible to have large disbudded blooms or glorious sprays almost at will.

Though details have been given in Chapter 3 on the correct taking of cuttings, it will be as well to point out here that gardeners who do not have a greenhouse can increase stock by (a) dividing old stools, (b) using rooted suckers from the stems, or (c) taking cuttings in a cold frame.

In the case of (a) the plants are left out each winter and it is hoped that they will not be killed by frost and wet. In early May they are lifted and when split into two or three the plants are put out where they are to flower in the summer. The resultant blooms are not as good, however, as those grown on plants from cuttings. In the north of the country it may be necessary to protect outdoor plants with glass cloches or Access frames in the winter.

In the case of rooted suckers, these are detached from old stock in early May and planted where they are to grow. These old stools may need some glass protection in winter, in the north, to make certain that the suckers are not killed off.

If you have cold frames, put a 3-in. layer of fairly fine ashes in the bottom of one of them, for drainage, and over this place a 2-in. layer of Alex No-Soil Compost. Make this really firm and level and then apply over the top an $\frac{1}{8}$-in. layer of really sharp silver sand; press this down level with a wooden presser. Have the frame ready by about 15 February so that the cuttings may be dibbled in a day later, 1 in. square. The compost used should be just moist, so it is a good idea to water it thoroughly through the fine rose of a can before the sharp sand is put on top.

As it is impossible, as a rule, to obtain cuttings in the middle of February from outdoor stools, it is advisable to cut down the

old chrysanthemum plants to within 6 in. of soil level in early
November, and then to plant them in a mixture of soil and sedge
peat in equal parts in a cold frame. The various varieties should
be kept separate and must be well labelled. Don't allow the
stools in the frame to be injured by frost; whenever there is a
serious frosty period, put not only three or four sheets of newspaper over the stools inside the frame, but also sacks or sacking
over the glass light of the frame. The moment the frost has gone
and it is bright again, the sacking may be removed and later on
the newspaper as well. Stools protected in this way in a cold
frame should produce young shoots which can be taken as cuttings in the middle of February.

To return to the cuttings in the frame, these should take a
month or five weeks to root and it is necessary to be extremely
careful not to water over the plants but only between them. Be
sparing with the water, for a sodden compost will not encourage
quick rooting. At the end of the month, it should be possible to
consider lifting the rooted cuttings so that they can be planted
into a third frame, this time 4 in. apart.

We have now come to about 20 March. The cuttings are
rooted and are now planted in their new frame, which is made
up in a similar way to the first one except that this time the No-
Soil Compost must be 4 in. deep when firm. This time, also, the
standard plant foods provided with the compost should be
added. Transplant the cuttings firmly, apply water between the
rows afterwards (as advised before), put the frame light into
position and leave completely closed for three or four days. After
that a little ventilation can be given at the top or bottom depending on the direction of the wind. The plants merely want fresh
air – they don't want a draught blowing in on them.

Gradually the plants are hardened off in this frame – that is to
say, more and more ventilation is given – until about 15 April.
The glass frame light may be taken off altogether during the day
when the weather is mild. Later on in the month it may be possible to leave the frame off altogether, night and day, so that the
plants are sturdy and so completely hardened off that they can
be planted out at the end of the month in the south (and even
earlier in places like Devon and Cornwall), and by 15 May in
the north.

To recap, therefore, the programme is as follows:

15 November   lift stools and put in frame 1
15 February   take cuttings from stools in frame 1 and dibble
               out in frame 2

| 15 March | plant rooted cuttings from frame 2 into frame 3 |
| 15 May | plant out hardened-off plants in open where they are to flower |

Of course, one cannot stick to these dates slavishly, but it is a help to beginners to have some definite dates to go by.

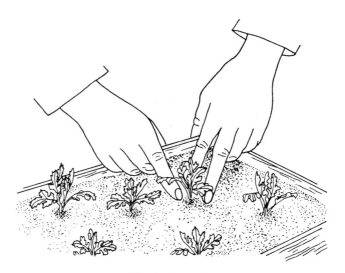

Firming in cuttings

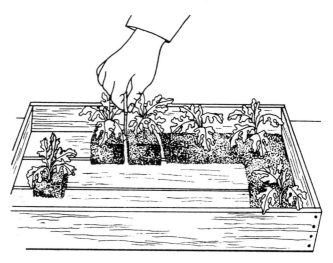

Chrysanthemum plants in soil blocks

Potting Up the Cuttings

Those who intend to go in for growing chrysanthemums for show should know that some of the best exhibitors, instead of planting the cuttings out in frames in March, pot them up individually into 3-in. plastic pots using Alex No-Soil Compost. This potting up is done about six weeks after the cuttings are inserted in their boxes (see Chapter 3). The cuttings growing in standard seed boxes are watered well early the day before. On the day of potting, the gardener takes a largish sharp knife and passes it down one way between the plants, through the compost, and then between the plants the other way, so that the compost is divided up into little squares containing the roots of the plants. If preferred, the side of the box may be removed so that the whole square of compost will slide out, and then the plants may be carefully separated.

Obtain a bag of No-Soil Compost, tip it out on to the potting bench or on to a wooden tray put on to the greenhouse staging. Water the compost with a fine rose on the can, turning it from time to time with a clean trowel or spade as you do this, so that it is just moist. If you are going to use a clay pot, it must be thoroughly scrubbed in clean water first, and a crock must be put over the hole in the bottom for drainage. The modern plastic pot will not need a crock because of its special drainage holes, but if it has been used before it will need to be washed clean in cold water.

Put the compost into the pots and press it down with the fingers so that it is fairly firm and so that it is 1 in. from the top rim. Take the rooted cutting, set it in the middle of the pot on the compost and spread out the roots. With one hand put in more compost to cover the roots and turn the pot in the other hand as you do so, and of course keep the plant upright. Press this compost down with the fingers. The pot should now be filled to within $\frac{1}{2}$ in. of the top. It helps if you tap the pot lightly from time to time while the compost is being put in, to make the compost settle down evenly.

Now place the firmly potted chrysanthemums on the staging of the greenhouse as close to one another as possible. Don't be tempted to over-water them at this stage, and if they should seem to flag just spray a little water overhead with a syringe. Watch out for greenfly and if it appears add liquid derris to the water when syringing overhead. Give the greenhouse a fair amount of ventilation so that the plants are not grown soft, and aim to be able to put these plants out into a cold frame about 5

April for the final hardening off. When the planting-out time comes, the ball of compost is carefully knocked out of the pot, and if there is a crock this is removed. A suitable sized hole having been made with a trowel, the plant is firmed in well in the place where it is going to grow and flower.

A Possible Potting On

There is even one further stage which the most successful exhibitors adopt, and that is to pot on the plants from 3-in. pots into 5-in. pots on or about 5 April. No-Soil Compost is again used and it is possible to stir in more of the plant foods as instructed on the container when the compost is bought. This time sufficient of the compost is put in the bottom of the clean 5-in. pot (which once again should be crocked if it is made of clay) so that when the ball of soil from the 3-in. pot is stood on that its top is within 1 in. of the rim of the new pot.

All that has to be done now is to put more compost around the ball of soil and ram it in firmly. A wooden rammer shaped rather like a chisel and about 5 in. long may be used for this purpose. The reason for having the additional compost put in around the ball as firm as the compost in the ball itself, is so that the roots of the plants will grow into it. It should be emphasized that this potting on must be done firmly if the plant is to do well.

The plant in its 5-in. pot will be perhaps 6 or 7 in. tall. To keep it upright, tie it loosely to a thin cane at 2 in. and again at 5 in. from its base. After the potting and staking, put the plants out into a cold frame so that the pots are almost touching one another, and only water when it is absolutely necessary. There is no need to put on the frame lights to cover them except on an evening when the BBC gives a serious frost warning. The plants in their 5-in. pots should be ready for planting out where they are to grow on about 15 May.

Preparation of the Site

Whether the plants have been raised in frames or in the greenhouse, successful results cannot be achieved unless time and trouble are taken with the preparation of the soil in which the plants are to grow. The best flowers seem to come from a light or medium loam rich in humus which is about 15 in. deep. Fork over the ground lightly, at the same time adding powdery compost or sedge peat at the rate of about 30 lb per square yard, plus a fish fertilizer with a 10 per cent potash content at 4 oz to the square yard. Some experts fork in ten full barrowloads of compost for every hundred plants of chrysanthemums grown.

Liming

Chrysanthemums do best on a soil which is slightly acid, that is
to say, where the pH is 6·5. It is a simple matter to test the soil
with a BDH Soil Indicator. If lime is needed carbonate of lime is
applied as a top dressing after the digging has been completed.
Many gardeners who don't want to bother to test the soil apply
half a pound of carbonate of lime per square yard as a routine
dressing each year. It wouldn't, however, be necessary to do this
in cases where soil is known to be chalky or limey.

The digging of the chrysanthemum ground should be done in
December and January and the ground should be left rough for
the frosts and cold winds to act on. There's no need to go near
the plot until, say, 5 April when the soil may be raked level and
made firm. This firming is very necessary in the case of light
sandy soils and it may be done if necessary with a roller. A fortnight before planting, apply the fish fertilizer evenly all over the
bed and rake it in very lightly.

Time to Plant

It is very difficult to be precise about times of planting. Many
experts in the south, for instance, who win prizes at Shows, do
not start to plant out of doors until 10 May, and continue until
20 May. It must be remembered, however, that exhibitors have
their plants in 5-in. pots. Normally, planting would be done,
perhaps, during the third week of April in the south, about 15
May in the midlands and 25 May in the north.

It is inadvisable to plant, however, unless the soil is in the
right condition. It must not be sodden with water, for you can
never plant firmly in muddy soil. It may be necessary, therefore,
to wait a few days for the soil to dry out. Planting times are often
different in the east and west of England, and there are warm
gardens on the west coast of Scotland, for instance, which are far
warmer than some on the east coast of southern England.
Please, therefore, adjust your planting to suit your own particular conditions.

The danger, of course, is frost; therefore do not plant early in
areas where late frosts are experienced unless you have to do so
because of the need to clear the frames. In that case, cover the
chrysanthemums with square glass Access frames until about
the end of May.

The holes for the plants are best made with a strong trowel
which has been flattened a little by beating with a wooden
mallet. It sounds peculiar to say this, but there is no doubt that

the blade of a normal trowel is a little too curved and a slightly flattened trowel makes a better hole to receive the ball of soil and the roots. Never allow an air pocket underneath the roots at planting time; this often happens, unfortunately, when planting is done with a dibber instead of a trowel.

Plant firmly but not too deeply. If the chrysanthemums are to be used as cut flowers, have the beds 4 ft 6 in. wide and then allow for a path 2 ft wide, another 2-ft path and so on. Within the bed four rows should be planted 18 in. apart. Drive 6-ft chestnut stakes into the corners of the beds. Between two of these stakes attach a 5-ft-long crossbar, $1\frac{1}{2}$ in. by $1\frac{1}{2}$ in., with wire. Fix a crossbar to the posts at either end of the bed and then arrange old government telephone wires so that they are stretched tightly 18 in. apart across from one crossbar to the other. Between these wires 4-ply fillis may be tied, thus forming 18-in. squares through which the plants may grow.

The purpose of this special square wire contraption is that it should be adjustable as the plants grow. It may start off, for instance, at 18 in. from soil level and may end at 4 ft from soil level. Instead of the wires and string, many people now use the very effective Weldmesh square wires which are available in suitable lengths.

Growers who are going to exhibit their plants may grow them in beds no wider than 18 in., with the two rows planted 18-in. apart. A 2-ft path is then left between the two rows, before planting another two rows 18 in. apart, leaving another 2-ft path, and so on. Instead of having wires to support the plants, 4-ft canes are used, the cane being pushed into position at the side of the hole before the planting is done.

Because Show plants are often grown on into 5-in. pots, a larger hole is necessary into which the ball of soil may fit snugly. Once again, plant firmly. This can best be done, perhaps, by pushing the trowel into the soil 2 in. away from the original hole and pressing the earth inwards towards the ball of soil containing the plant roots. Immediately after planting, the young chrysanthemum plant must be tied to the cane at a point 2 in. above soil level. As the plants grow, further ties are made, with raffia or green twine wrapped loosely around the stems of the plants and tightly around the cane itself.

Watering

It is easiest to plant when the soil is just moist, because if the plants are well watered the day before transplanting, it shouldn't be necessary to water them in, *in situ*. If there should be a very dry spell, the gardener should syringe the plants over in the morning and again in the evening. It is far better to get the plants to seek out their own moisture than to water the roots and, so to speak, make them lazy. Ten days after planting some water may be given if it continues dry. It should be applied through the fine rose of a can. Sprinklers that give artificial rain are ideal and can be left in position for half an hour or more. Never attempt what the amateur gardener calls the daily dose.

Hoeing
Use the Dutch hoe, so that the top $\frac{1}{2}$ in. of soil can be cut through with a really sharp blade. Walk backwards as the work proceeds and the footmarks will then be hoed out. Continue the hoeing until the last week in July. Hoeing not only continues to control weeds but also creates a dust mulch, which helps to keep the moisture in the ground.

Birds and Pests
In some districts, birds can be a nuisance for the first month after planting, and this is especially true in the case of many town gardens. It is said that they come for the greenfly, but many gardeners believe it is sheer devilment. The leaves are stripped and just left lying about. There is an amazing product called Scaraweb which may be stretched between the wires and bamboos in a few moments and, because of its spider's-web-like appearance, keeps the sparrows away.

Control the greenfly by spraying with liquid derris once a week or so from the middle of May onwards. A good overhead spray with this organic insecticide not only controls the pests but also freshens up the leaves of the plants.

Tying Up
In the case of plants growing in beds, there is no tying up to do, for the string and wire mesh does the necessary supporting at the right time. In cases where the gardener wants to grow his chrysanthemums for show, it is necessary to have an individual cane for each branch, or break as it is usually called. This should be pushed into the soil at an angle of 75 degrees. When tying the branches to the canes the raffia or green twine should be looped around the stem and then tightly wrapped twice around the cane. The stem must never be tied tightly to a cane or it may snap off in a high wind. Decide on the number of branches to be

grown per plant and this will give you the number of canes to be used. Any laterals in excess of the number required must be cut off carefully.

Earwigs

In the past earwigs have been a great nuisance, ruining the roots of plants. It may be necessary to block up all the holes in the bamboos with putty to prevent the creatures from hibernating there. Derris dust must be used along the bottoms of the hedgerows in May and then around the bottoms of plants in June and, maybe, again in July.

Mulching

Early-flowering Chrysanthemums much appreciate a top dressing of medium grade sedge peat at the beginning of June. This should be put on at least 1 in. deep all over the ground where the plants are growing. This is to keep the roots cool and to provide some extra humus which the plants love. Furthermore, it is invariably at the beginning of July that Early-flowering Chrysanthemums start to make new surface roots and mulching will preserve these. Feed the plants with a fish fertilizer at 3 oz to the square yard before the peat is applied. (This application of peat is particularly valuable in the case of show blooms of Exhibition varieties.)

Stopping

Details of the times of stopping appear in Chapter 5, but the gardener must remember that the pinching out of the growing point of the plant may have to be done after planting. It is always said that it takes about seven weeks from the time of stopping to the appearing of the flower buds at the tips of the branches, and a further seven weeks for that bud to blossom out into a perfect flower. These are merely general figures to bear in mind.

Feeding, however, plays a part in either delaying or hastening the development of flowers. A starved plant flowers earlier, on the whole, than one that has been fed well, especially if nitrogen is given. Phosphates, however, have a tendency to bring flowering forward, and some chrysanthemum growers therefore use bone meal liberally.

When plants have been stopped the laterals start to develop. These breaks, as they are called, may number five, six or seven, or, in some cases, twelve. Growers who are going in for showing will probably leave only four branches on each plant, but for normal cut-flower work eight or nine good branches will be ideal.

Feeding

One of the best ways of feeding chrysanthemum plants is by means of Marinure or Farmura, because these contain all the essential plant nutriments in correct proportions, together with trace elements. Organic liquid fertilizers are speedy in action and are quite easy to use. When dry feeds are given it is necessary to water them in when it doesn't rain. Generally speaking, feed Early-flowering Chrysanthemums from 1 June onwards once a fortnight, it being best to give a little and often. In wet seasons, give a fertilizer with a high potash content and in sunny, dry seasons, an organic fertilizer with a high nitrogen content. I use, for instance, Marinure with high potash in a dull summer, and ordinary Marinure in a droughty year.

It must be remembered that these organic foods are given in addition to the well-rotted dung or good compost that is dug in during the late autumn or early winter. Sometimes it is necessary to apply small quantities of Epsom salts (magnesium sulphate) at the rate of 1 oz to the square yard, but only when the margins of the leaves appear yellow.*

Note the bud at the end of the stem. All the side flowering buds have been removed

This medicine, as it must be called, should be well watered in when applied to the ground. It is seldom, however, that magnesium trouble occurs when sufficient compost is given in the first place.

Disbudding

The whole purpose of disbudding is to allow the plant to concentrate its energies on the top flower bud, and thus to have one really large specimen rather than a number of small ones. The gardener uses the term 'securing the bud', and to do this operation he carefully removes, with thumb and forefinger or with a sharp knife, all the side buds or side shoots that are developing near the terminal.

Some people say it is important not to remove all the side buds on the same day, because when this is done a distorted main bud occurs. I myself, however, have never had any trouble after doing this. In fact, the sooner the disbudding is done, the better. If the side buds are left too long, then the main flower

A garden tub of Spray Chrysanthemums

* This seldom happens when compost is made properly at home and is used as a brown powdery mulch.

bud will tend to be flatter in shape than it should be. Generally speaking, disbudding starts in the second week of July and with Earlies may continue until the end of the first week of August.

Laterals and Suckers

Once the bud has been secured, the plant knows that it cannot develop any extension growth. It may, therefore, try and use up its surplus energy by producing laterals in the axils of the leaves or by throwing up suckers from ground level. Do not allow the chrysanthemum to dissipate the elaborated sap in this way, so cut out the laterals and suckers immediately they are seen, so that the energy of the plants will go into the production of perfect blooms.

Protection

Although Early-flowering Chrysanthemums will normally grow happily out of doors without any protection at all, it is often necessary in the north and in parts of England where there are September gales, to use some method of protecting the plants. Dutch Light covers would be ideal. Alternatively hessian, coarse coconut matting or hop lew could be used, nailed on to posts on the windy sides of chrysanthemum beds in order to minimize the gale force and prevent the bruising and damaging of the flowers.

People who grow chrysanthemums in towns and cities have to put up with smuts from chimney smoke and they may have to put over the beds a temporary roof of polythene spread on a framework. This will also give protection from excessive rain. Top protection of this kind will often prevent frost damage also. In some gardens I have seen individual plants covered with umbrellas made of plastic, held on posts 6 in. above the flowers. For Show purposes some people use paper or polythene bags to cover individual blooms towards the end of their life. Paper bags must be made of greaseproof paper, and when inflated must hold the bloom easily without touching its sides. Good bags measure about 10 in. square. Do not attempt to cover until the flowers are well out. (see page 67.)

Some Dwarf Pompon varieties that grow well in pots: (top l. to r.) Cameo, Denise, Salmon Fairie (bottom l. to r.) Bronze Fairie, Purple Fairie

The simplest method of covering for protection is to drive in posts 2 in. square at the corners of the beds. These posts must be 7 ft 6 in. long so that they may be knocked 18 in. into the soil. If the beds are long, then posts must be driven in every 10 ft. From the top of the post a galvanized wire must be stretched tightly and from this wire a curtain of hessian may be hung. The roof

Chrysanthemums outside under temporary Dutch Light covers, to protect
them from the frost

may be made of butter muslin or of thin plastic sheeting, to complete the tent-like effect and protect the plants. A plastic roof
must always slope a little so that the rain will run off.

As the Flowers Turn In

As the chrysanthemum blooms start to open, watch out for the
little black thrips (or thunder bugs as they are sometimes
called) which cause tiny brown spots or streaks on the petals. If
you see some, spray with liquid nicotine on a warm day, using
$\frac{1}{4}$oz of nicotine to a $2\frac{1}{2}$-gallon bucket of water, plus a dessertspoonful of soap flakes.

The flowers last better if the plants are watered well the day

*Intended for showing, this chrysanthemum is protected in its final growing
stage from frost and excessive rain by a loose, polythene bag*

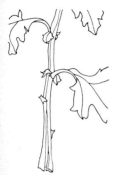

*Splitting the bottom of
the stem before putting
the flower in water*

before the stems are cut. Immediately after cutting, stand the
stems up to their necks in deep water in a cool shed or room for
eight hours. After this, strip off the bottom few leaves, slit the
bottom of the stem up 1 in. with a sharp knife to help let in the
water, and then put them in vases in the house.

7 The Possibilities of 'Lifting In'

The term 'lifting in' is used to indicate the digging up of chrysanthemum plants in the late autumn in order to bring them into the greenhouse and plant them there. It is a particularly popular idea in the north of England where frosts may be expected round about 24 or 25 September. The October- and, maybe, even November-flowering varieties will therefore be grown out of doors in the normal way, with the minimum of work, while the greenhouse is occupied with tomatoes.

The lifting in of chrysanthemums may be described as an expedient for busy men and women. There is little doubt that the plants would do better in large pots, but pot plants need regular watering, the pots have to be stood on a well-drained coarse ash base, and the bamboo supports must be tied to wires in case the plants blow over. All this takes time and money. The lifted-in plants cannot be said to do as well as those in pots, but they succeed well enough, and if you cannot have cake, it is pleasant enough to have really good bread and jam!

Various expedients have been adopted in respect of these 'lifted-in' plants. In the first place it is most important to make certain that the soil is rich in organic matter so that when the plants are dug up the soil, with its high humus content, clings to the roots. Secondly, it is a very good thing in a dry period to water the ground well the day before lifting, so that the leaves of the plants are really turgid, having taken in all the moisture they need. Thirdly, it is a good idea to plunge a sharp spade into the ground 4 in. away from the plants on all sides, so preparing a 'square' which will be easier to lift a week later. The plunging of the spade perpendicularly cuts off any fibrous roots outside the block of soil thus made, and encourages new root hairs to be produced within this area. Thus when the chrysanthemums are carefully lifted a week later, the square of soil comes up compactly, ready for putting in position at the same depth in the greenhouse.

Some firms have produced wide, meshed-wire baskets. These are sunk into the soil and the chrysanthemums are planted in them. Because the top of the basket is 1 in. or so below soil level, normal hoeings can be carried out in the summer out of doors. Furthermore, the bamboos can be pushed into the soil through the baskets in order to give the plants the necessary support.

When the time comes for lifting, a fork is plunged into the ground just outside the area taken up by the basket and the roots inside their wire container are lifted without any difficulty. The plants with their baskets are set out in the soil in the greenhouse at the end of the season, and the baskets recovered for use again another season. I have been able to use wire baskets again and again, successfully, for eight or nine years.

Some gardeners like to plant chrysanthemums for lifting in threes, in a triangle, each plant being 1 ft away from the next, and a distance of 18 in. being allowed between triangles. The spade is then plunged into the soil, as already advised, around the triangle, fourteen days before the day of lifting. The three plants should come up in one really large ball of soil and they can then be taken by wheelbarrow into the greenhouse, for planting there. It has been argued that although the triangle method may be good, the big ball of soil thus produced is far too heavy. In addition, because the plants have to grow so close together they grow drawn and soft.

I like to have the chrysanthemums planted on a 20 in. square principle, each plant having a good bamboo for support. Before planting, well-rotted compost is forked in at two bucketsful to the square yard, and after planting sedge peat is applied as a top dressing mulch at one bucketful to the square yard. In exposed gardens, some support must be given to the plants which are to be lifted in. For this purpose 6-ft posts may be driven into the ground at the end of each row with a strong wire stretched in between. The tops of the bamboos may then be tied to the wire.

Before lifting in, on about 20 September in the north and 5 or 6 October in the south, spray the plants thoroughly with Karathane in order to prevent mildew and with a liquid derris-pyrethrum wash to kill insect pests. The cutting down (sometimes called cutting back) of the plants should be done fourteen days beforehand and a thorough watering of the area two days before that. In the greenhouse, a trench should be prepared of the right width to take the ball of soil, and when the first trench is filled with plants the soil from the next trench should be put on the top and trodden in well. Thus the chrysanthemums are

planted trench by trench 1 ft apart. Every four rows an 18-in.
pathway should be left, to allow for easy picking.

Once the plants are in position and have been trodden in well,
a thorough watering should be given. For two days after this,
keep the greenhouse closed in order to check transpiration until
the plants get over the move. After this open the ventilators
night and day for fourteen days and keep the temperature of the
house at 50 degrees F.

Don't think it extraordinary to be asked to keep up the heat in
the greenhouse with the ventilators open. What is needed is a
buoyant atmosphere to ensure that the plants are free from
mildew and that the flowers are not 'damped off' in the centre.
Of course, as the nights get colder the ventilators will be closed
in the late afternoon. Keen chrysanthemum growers should be
prepared to give a certain amount of ventilation during the day
unless the weather is very frosty.

When the plants recover from the move they may be fed once
a week with diluted Marinure or Farmura until the flowers start
to show their colour. If it is necessary to control pests and diseases in the greenhouse despite the spraying that has been done
before the plants were lifted in, then it is advisable to burn one of
the modern 'smokes' that are made for greenhouse fumigation.
These can be obtained from any good horticultural chemist.

Varieties

There are certain chrysanthemum varieties which seem particularly suited to these lifting-in methods. The leaves show the
minimum amount of flagging and the plants recover quickly
from the move and flower well.

Name	*Description*	*Time of Flowering*
Balcombe Perfection (and Sports)	Incurved, chestnut	November–December
Christmas Carol	red with gold reverse	November
Christmas Wine	Incurved, scarlet crimson	December
Fred Shoesmith	beautiful white	November–December
Goldplate	Reflexed, large, amber	October–December
Marigold	bright orange spray	November–December
Minstrel	rose-pink spray	November–December
Shirley Late Red	Reflexed, Indian red	December
Yellow Fred Shoesmith	Incurved, clear yellow	November–December

8 Growing Chrysanthemums in Pots

The great advantage of growing the later type of chrysanthemums in pots is that regular, steady growth is achieved, resulting in the best type of bloom. In pots the plant roots can be well watered and, of course, properly fed. Generally speaking, the struck cuttings are first potted up into 3-in. pots and later, when they are well grown, into 5-in. pots, and finally into 9- or 10-in. pots.

There are three types of pot normally used by amateur gardeners: (a) the usual clay pot, (b) the new plastic pot, and (c) the whalehide pot which only lasts a year. Some gardeners, instead of using 9-in. pots, use square biscuit tins, first knocking a hole or two in the bottom to give good drainage.

It doesn't matter much what the container is, providing it is absolutely clean, is not made of some substance that will inhibit growth, and is sufficiently sturdy and strong not to fall to pieces either as the plant grows or as the containers are lifted into the greenhouse.

If normal clay pots are used year after year it does pay to immerse them in boiling water for ten to fifteen minutes, to ensure that they are free from disease germs, and then to scrub them well inside and outside. The plants should then have a good start that season. Any broken crocks used in the bottom of the pots should be boiled for ten minutes also.

Into the 3-in. Pot
The cutting has been struck, it has produced a number of roots, it has been hardened off in a frame and is now ready to be potted up into its 3-in. pot. Alex No-Soil Compost will be used for this purpose, or John Innes Potting Compost 1. It will be just moist, and after a large crock has been placed concave side downwards over the drainage hole the compost will be put in and the base of the pot tapped lightly on the table or bench. If the pot is half filled first of all, the well-rooted young plant can be placed in the

centre of the pot on to the firmed compost and more of this compost can be poured in around the plant, a little tapping being done again to settle the compost evenly. The compost will then be pressed down with two fingers until its level is ½ in. below the rim of the pot.

The 3-in. pots now go into frames where they get the normal protection from frosts and excessive rain. There they are syringed overhead with clean water about ten o'clock each morning and after ten days the plants may need a good watering. By ventilating the frames well and giving the plants plenty of air, strong and sturdy growth should be achieved. By the end of April or the beginning of May, in the south, and the beginning of May in the north, the lights can be removed altogether.

Gardeners who do not want to put their plants out into a frame may stand them on the staging of the greenhouse at a temperature of not more than 40 degrees F. Care should be taken to provide a good shingle or ash base, both in the frame and on the staging, to ensure perfect drainage. Some people use black polythene in the bottom of the frame to prevent the roots growing into the soil or ashes below. If the plants are in the greenhouse, open the ventilator on all favourable occasions. As the weather gets warmer it may be possible to stop heating the house altogether.

In the case of Late- and Semi-late-flowering varieties it is best if the well-struck cuttings are potted up into their 3-in. pots in the third or fourth week of February. When this is done the young plants are seldom elongated and leggy. The first potting up, incidentally, should not be too firm. There is always a tendency for the ball of soil to compact itself. Therefore, when potting on from a 3-in. pot to a 5-in. pot, the new compost put around the original ball of soil must be rammed. If this is not done, the original ball of soil containing the roots will not be moistened with watering because the water will flow down and loosen the compost on the outside.

The plants in their 3-in. pots need a fair amount of looking after as they grow – it may be necessary, for instance, to space the plants out a little more. When they get bushy, i.e. ten days or a week before they are potted up into 5-in. pots, they may need spacing out to 5 in. apart. Watering must be carefully done, for the compost must be kept sufficiently moist for the leaves not to flag, and yet it must never be sodden or the air will be driven out and then the leaves will flag for that reason. If the plants are in cold frames in March and early April, it may be necessary to cover them with sheets of brown paper in addition to the lights, to make certain that they are not killed by frost. No water, however, should be given during such a period.

Plants that are stood on the staging of a cool house must never be allowed to be in a draught. Ventilate on one side of the house only – ventilation on both sides may encourage a howling gale to pass through. Sometimes it is advisable to turn the pots round, if there is more light on one side of a frame or greenhouse than on the other. Gardeners sometimes remove a pot from one end of the house or frame, move all the plants up one, and then put plant No. 1 at the end of the row. During this move the pots can be turned around also.

Into the 5-in. Pot

After the plants have been growing well in their 3-in. pots for some time, they will be potted on into 5-in. pots. Do not do this until the roots are filling the 3-in. pots and starting to curl round the ball of soil. Pot on, therefore, before the roots become matted or, as the gardener says, 'pot bound'. The time for potting on may differ from one year to another, but if the potting up into 3-in. pots was carried out during the third week of February, the plants should be ready to pot up into 5-in. pots about the third week in March. If, however, the work is done during the fourth week in February then the first potting on will take place at the end of March. This time it is usual to use John Innes Compost 3 or Alex No-Soil Compost 3.

Look over the plants carefully as the potting on is done, and if there is any sign of green or black aphids dip the plants, pot and all, into a bucket of water containing nicotine and soap flakes. (The formula is ¾oz nicotine to a 2½-gallon bucketful of water, plus 1 dessertspoonful of soap flakes.) Having done the dipping, turn the pot upside down, put two fingers on either side of the stem of the plant, and tap the rim of the pot on the table or bench. It will then come away cleanly and the crock may be removed.

As mentioned earlier on, the potting up at this stage must be firmer than in the 3-in. pot. Put a large piece of broken crock curve downwards over the drainage holes and add a small handful of smaller crocks. Over the crocks place a small handful of rough sedge peat and then sufficient compost to fill the pot to about the half-way level. Firm this compost and stand the ball of soil in the centre, holding the plant in position with the left hand while taking up new compost with the right. Having put compost all around the outside of the ball of soil, take a stick about 5 in. long and about the thickness of a broom handle and ram the compost down well. It helps if this stick is slightly tapered at the end. Do not over-ram at this stage because there is yet one more potting on to be done and the last one, naturally, is the firmest one of all.

When the plant has been potted up, not only should new compost be underneath the plant and on the two sides, but also covering the top of the ball of soil by about ½ in. Further, the final soil level should be 1 in. from the rim of the pot. Never bury the plant deeper than 1 in. in the new compost, or root rotting may take place.

When ready the pots can go back to the cold frames and stand close together, rim to rim. Put the lights over them for three or four days to help them recover properly from the potting-on operation; at the end of this period it should be possible to remove the glass lights altogether. It should not be necessary to water heavily because the compost used should be in the right condition, that is to say, just moist: not so wet that when squeezed some moisture oozes out, and yet not so dry that the handful of soil falls to pieces when the hand is opened after the squeezing. If it retains its shape it is in the correct condition.

When the pots go back into their frames, it is advisable to tie the plant loosely to a 2-ft-long bamboo to keep it upright. (Bamboo canes, by the way, last much longer if they are dipped in Rentokil preserving fluid for an hour or so before using.) If the plants have been on the staging of the greenhouse, then they must go back there for a week or ten days after they have been potted up into 5-in. pots. Only at the end of this period should they go into the cold frames.

Don't coddle the plants, whether in the greenhouse or the frame. See that they get plenty of light and air, so that not only will the stems be sturdy but also that the leaves will have a nice dark green colour.

Stopping Pot Plants

The charts concerned with stopping in Chapter 5 should be carefully studied. About the end of April, and even a little earlier in some cases, it will be necessary to pinch out the growing points of the flowers. In cases where the blooms are going to be taken on the second crown buds, some of the Reflexed Decoratives will need their first stopping about 15 April.

About this time most stopping will be done in any case, unless the variety is one which breaks naturally. Chrysanthemum catalogues of the best nurserymen invariably indicate when stopping is required, as well as making it quite clear whether it is best to allow the plants to flower on the first or second crown.

Into the 9-in. Pot

Having encouraged the plants to grow on quietly in their 5-in. pots, and having seen to it that they are watered regularly, it should be possible to pot them up into their 9-in. pots during the last two weeks of May or, at the latest, the first two weeks of June. If, because of weather conditions, it is necessary to delay the final potting on, be sure to water the pots once a week with dilute Marinure or Farmura, or to give each pot as much fish manure as will go easily on to a ten-pence piece. This can be watered in if the weather is dry.

Most people today aim at standardization, and so instead of putting the weaker growing varieties into 9-in. pots and the stronger growing kinds into 10-in. pots, they adopt 9-in. pots for all. Once again, all the pots used must be clean. It is best to submerge them in boiling water for ten minutes or a quarter of an hour. Let the pots and crocks dry out and then place one large crock over the drainage hole of each pot and put a handful or two of coarse sedge peat over the top. Now fill the pot half-way with John Innes Potting Compost 4 or Alex No-Soil Compost 4, so that when the ball of soil from the 5-in. pot is in position there will be a 2-in. space left at the top for watering and feeding.

Now, holding the plant with the left hand, put plenty of new compost around the ball and ram it down, this time very firmly. Keep turning the pot round, adding more compost as you do so, and keep on ramming. Some gardeners cover the top of the ball of soil with $\frac{1}{2}$ in. of the new compost, pressing this in well also. Now push in two bamboos on opposite sides of the pot, slanting outwards – remember that the plant is going to spread at the top. The height of the canes must equal the height of the plants, anything from 4 to 6 ft. Label each pot correctly, give the plant a good watering and then stand the pot where it is to be during the summer.

The Standing Ground

As the chrysanthemums have got to grow quietly but definitely in their pots all through the summer and early autumn, out of doors, it is necessary to provide a sheltered level site on which the pots can be stood. This, preferably, should be as near the

The stems of this fine variety, Connie Mayhew, are tied loosely to bamboo canes for support

greenhouse as possible so that there is the minimum of cartage when the time comes for the pots to be taken under glass, in late September or early October.

If the site is not naturally sheltered, then it is a good idea to provide a windbreak, made of coarse hessian or sacking about 6 ft wide. This can then be nailed on to strong posts driven into the ground 4 ft or so away from the standing ground area.

The site chosen should be covered 2 in. deep with clinkers that have been crushed and then rolled level. It is important to provide these for three reasons: (1) to provide perfect drainage, (2) to prevent any rooting through the bottom of the pots into the soil below, and (3) to prevent worms working their way up along the soil and through the drainage holes into the compost. If plenty of good rough ashes are rolled down level, there should be very little trouble with weeds. I have stood the pots out on concrete slabs, successfully, and have seen some growers stand the pots on a grass sward.

Some gardeners object to putting down ashes, thus making a permanent standing ground, and prefer to use black Fablothene laid down on the ground in 4-ft-wide strips after the soil has been rolled level and firm. The pots then stand on the black plastic which, of course, prevents worms from tunnelling through and ensures that weeds are controlled. For drainage, however, it is not as good as coarse ashes.

Whether ashes, slabs or grass are used, or even black Fablothene, it is convenient to stand the pots like sentries, back to back, in a series of double rows. These rows should run from north to south. Normally the pots in the two rows should be allowed to touch one another, but if the flowers are being grown for exhibition, the double rows should be arranged 10 in. away from one another. This latter scheme does mean that the gardener has to give up a great deal of room for a standing ground.

Normally, then, there will be a double row of pots standing next to one another, then a 3-ft path, another two rows of pots, another 3-ft path and so on. By allowing for the pathways the gardener is easily able to disbud, spray, feed and water the plants.

Supporting and Tying
Although suggestions have been made earlier about erecting hessian for protection against winds, it should also be said that this is only necessary in very exposed situations. Chrysanthemums like plenty of fresh air and sunshine, and if the plants

are well supported with bamboos and the tops of these are tied to wires, the pots will not blow over and the plants will not be harmed by a normal amount of wind.

Bamboo canes 5 ft long should be soaked in Rentokil preservative for at least an hour before use. One cane should be pushed carefully into each pot as close to the base of the plant as possible. It is easy to say that the bamboos should be pushed in without damaging the roots of the plants, but to do this after the final potting up is impossible. Those who grow for exhibition often use three bamboos pushed in at an angle of 75 degrees, but this is a refinement and not absolutely necessary.

To support the wires to which the bamboos are going to be tied, a stout post must be driven in at the end of each double row and in the middle. A wooden T-piece 2 in. square should be nailed on to each post at a point 4 ft 6 in. above ground level. From the outside of the Ts, strong wires should be stretched tightly so that they run parallel to the pots below. These wires must be absolutely tight and the tops of the canes should be tied to them.

It only remains now for the branches of the plants to be tied loosely to the bamboo. The tie around the bamboo itself will be tight and around the stem loose. Most gardeners give a new tie every 6 in. as the plant grows, but others say that every 8 in. will do. Raffia can be used for the ties and this keeps better if it is soaked for two hours in green Rentokil before using. The alternative is to tie with green twine.

Gardeners who dislike using wooden posts, because the posts eventually rot, however carefully protected with green Rentokil, can buy the more expensive aluminium posts which have a T-piece put in position with a butterfly nut and bolt. The advantage of this scheme is that if the aluminium post is bored with holes every 6 in. the T-piece can be raised if the plants grow tall. Further, in the case of Dwarf-growing varieties like Loveliness which don't usually grow taller than 4 ft, the T-piece may be lowered.

The Second Stopping

As the plants grow, bear in mind that with some varieties it is necessary to stop them a second time. Look at the tables in Chapter 5 and scan the notes given in the various chrysanthemum catalogues. By the time the second stopping becomes necessary, from about the second week of June onwards, four good laterals will have developed. When these are stopped, ten or even twelve good flowering shoots should be possible. Stick to the general dates given, however, until you become an expert and then like to experiment on your own.

Weeding and Watering

Despite the fact that No-Soil Compost has been used, there are always weed seeds which blow on to the tops of the pots and start to grow. These weed seeds must be removed before they start to compete with the roots of the chrysanthemums. Take a bucket or trug basket, go down the rows, pull the weeds out and put them into the container, and at the end throw them on to the compost heap, where they can be sprinkled with a little fish fertilizer. Weeds not only rob plants of food but they can also become a breeding ground for pests and diseases.

While weeding, it is worth noting the unwanted growths or suckers that are growing up from the roots. These can be cut off with a sharp knife below soil level and can then go on to the compost heap with the weeds.

For the first ten days after the plants have been stood out on the standing ground, no watering should be necessary. After that period it will probably be necessary to water about once a week, and on each occasion a really good soaking should be given. The quickest way of doing this work is to fit a big rose to the end of a hose and then to walk slowly down the rows making certain that each pot is filled with water. Varieties with larger leaves or more leaves tend to ask for more water than plants with smaller or fewer leaves.

It is usually after the fourth watering that all the plants in the rows seem to ask for the same amount of water. At this time, if the weather is getting hotter and sunnier, it may be necessary to water every two days. In a very hot droughty August, I have found it necessary to water twice a day for a week or so – once early in the morning and again early in the evening.

Because watering takes such a lot of time, many people like to use what is called a watering harness. This is a rubber tube fitted at definite intervals with a special type of non-block nozzle. The end of the rubber tube is attached to a hose and the hose to a tap, so that when the tap is turned on, all the pots fitted with a harness and hose get an equal amount of water, drop by drop, with the minimum of labour. Explain to the firm selling the harness the general layout of the pots on the standing ground and they will provide the equipment to fit your layout.

Feeding

It is very difficult indeed to lay down firm rules on the subject of feeding, but there is little doubt that dilute liquid plant food may be given the moment the bulk of the roots has penetrated into the new compost in the large pots. Beginners may like to knock out one plant, a typical one preferably, to see whether the roots have worked their way through or not. Most beginners, as a rule, start feeding too late. If a date had to be given it would be about 20 June. From then on, one can feed every ten days right up to the end of September. Light top dressings of fish manure are given by some growers instead of liquid manure.

Tying

As they grow the branches must be tied to the canes, as has already been explained – a double twist around the bamboo and a loose tie round the stem. In the early stages this tying up may have to be done once a week. Branches must receive their first ties when they are 5 in. long. Tying is a useful operation because at the same time the gardener keeps a sharp look-out for diseases and pests and then, if necessary, takes some means of control. He can also remove laterals or side shoots that are not required.

Lifting in the Pots

When the date comes for lifting in, during the third week of September in the north or sometime in October in the south, see to it that the soil in the greenhouse is quite level. In very tall houses the pot plants may go on to the staging but normally they are stood on the ground so that they have plenty of head room. Take the trouble of removing any yellowing or diseased bottom leaves before bringing the plants under cover, and spray them with Karathane to control the mildew and Malathion to kill the insect pests.

Most gardening authors advise amateurs to give the pots a good watering before they are brought inside, but in my own gardens we do not water for four days beforehand, so that when the plants are moved the leaves are soft and flaccid and do not break off so easily as when they are turgid and stiff. The moment the plants are in position in the greenhouse, however, each pot is filled with water.

Various arrangements are adopted so that each individual plant can be looked after properly. Some gardeners give the plants a breathing space of 12 in. on all sides. Others economize in space by putting the pots in three rows touching one another, then leaving a 2-ft pathway between the first three rows and the next three rows, and so on. It depends very much on the size of the greenhouse as to what can be done.

Keep the temperature in the greenhouse at this time at about 50 degrees F but don't attempt to coddle. Aim to have a free circulation of air – the electrical or hot-water-pipe heat will keep the air in the house buoyant. Keep on feeding and watering as already advised and only allow the temperature to rise a little, as the flowers are opening out, if you want to open them out quickly. Never be frightened of opening the ventilators in the daytime unless it is foggy or really frosty, because humidity and mugginess in the greenhouse only encourages diseases.

From now on pests and diseases may be controlled by means of fumigation. Various 'smokes' may be bought for this purpose.

Varieties

It is impossible to include a full list of the best varieties for growing in pots in the greenhouse. In any case a list would soon get out of date. So I have listed twelve varieties, all of which are easy to grow, given the normal amount of attention.

Name	Description	Time of Flowering
Balcombe Perfection (and Sports)	Incurved, broad petals, bronze	November–December
Christmas Wine	Incurved, rich wine	December
Daily Mirror	Incurved, rich purple	November
Favourite (and Sports)	Reflexed, white	December
Fred Shoesmith (and Sports)	large ivory-white	November–December
Glorietta	Reflexed, lavender	November
Goldplate	Reflexed, orange-bronze	October–November
Mayford Perfection (and Sports)	large salmon-pink	November–December
Minstrel	rose-pink sprays	November–December
Princess Anne (and Sports)	Reflexed, pink	November
Shirley Late Red	Reflexed, Indian red	December
Shoesmith's Salmon (and Sports)	Reflexed, salmon	December–January

Princess Anne, a beautiful, medium-flowered, Reflexed, pink variety, particularly suitable for growing in pots in the greenhouse

9 Decorative Dwarf Pot Plants

A great deal of interest has been aroused in recent years in the Decorative dwarf pot Chrysanthemum. These chrysanthemums, which may not grow taller than 18 in. or so, can be ablaze with small blooms and so can be used effectively as decorative pot plants in the home. They are usually grown in 5-in. pots, preferably plastic, and the plants are treated in quite a different manner from the taller types.

There are five main types of chrysanthemum grown as pot plants: (1) the normal dwarf chrysanthemums Blanche Poitevine and Yellow Poitevine, (2) Cushion Koreans, (3) Pompons, (4) Charms, and (5) Mini-mums. With the last four types it is possible to have early varieties that bloom out of doors, i.e. Koreans and Pompons in July and August, and Charms and Mini-mums in September. (Fuller details of these varieties will be found in Chapters 15 and 16.) The object in this chapter is to deal with the types and varieties that can become good pot plants for the house.

Normal Dwarf Chrysanthemums

It is usual with these types to take the cuttings during late March and early April and to strike them in John Innes Compost 1 or Alex No-Soil Compost 1. Six cuttings should be dibbled in around the edge of the pot, this being placed on the staging of the greenhouse where it will get a certain amount of bottom heat. The moment these cuttings have rooted they should be potted up individually into 3-in. pots, again using John Innes Compost 1 or Alex No-Soil Compost 1.

It is possible to take cuttings from the stems of the plants as late as April or early May, and these can be dibbled into boxes containing Alex No-Soil Compost as advised in Chapter 3. This late striking of cuttings is usually welcomed by the gardener because the other young chrysanthemum plants are well out of the way by that time. When rooted these cuttings are potted up into 3-in. pots, as in the case of the cuttings struck late in March.

Potting On

When the plants are growing well in their 3-in. pots and the roots are starting to curl around the edge of the ball, potting on into 5-in. pots can be done, using John Innes Compost 3 or Alex No-Soil Compost 3. In some cases it is sufficient to have one plant per pot, but to make a more brilliant show with certain varieties three plants may be potted on into one 5-in. pot. The potting at this stage must be done fairly firmly.

Stopping and Timing

In order to keep the plants dwarf and to ensure the maximum number of blooms, it is usual to stop the plants twice and then to aim for twelve or thirteen good blooms on second crown buds. It is possible to get as many as fifteen flowers on shortish stems after the second stopping. With most ordinary chrysanthemums the growing points will be pinched out, but with the plants in 5-in. pots it is usual to cut back 1 in. or so of growth and sometimes more, in order to produce sturdy, bushy plants. At the first stopping four laterals may be allowed to develop and at the second stopping three or four per stem, making twelve to sixteen blooms in all.

One cannot be definite about the dates for stopping in respect of all varieties, but generally speaking with varieties like Mrs Mary Moran and Rose Poitevine, the first stopping is done about 15 May, and the second about 15 June.

General Care

These dwarf chrysanthemums in their 5-in. pots need the same kind of treatment as the taller kinds in their 9-in. pots. They are stood outside on ashes where they remain throughout the summer and early autumn. They have to be watered regularly, but, in addition, it helps if the leaves are syringed over once a week in the evening. It is best to space the plants out 15 in. apart because they will need plenty of room for development. Because the plants do not grow tall they will not need any post or wire supports – especially if they are firmly placed on the ashes.

Each plant will need a short bamboo, which should be soaked before use in Rentokil preservative for at least one hour. Push the bamboo into the centre of the pot and then, if it is really necessary, each stem may be looped loosely around and a tight tie made in the centre on to the cane.

Pests and Diseases

Because the plants are dwarfed and because there are large numbers of stems on a plant, there is usually more trouble from pests and diseases. Early in June spray with liquid derris, giving a second dose early in July. If mildew should occur spray with Karathane.

Liquid Feeds

Generally speaking, follow the instructions given in Chapter 4. Marinure, with its high potash content, will make the leaves firmer and therefore not so likely to be attacked by diseases.

Varieties

A number of varieties have proved particularly suitable for growing as dwarf specimen plants in 5-in. pots. The following can be recommended:

Name	Description
Blanche Poitevene (and Sports)	Decorative, white
Marie Morin (and Sports)	Incurved, white
Mini-mum Charisma	Anemone-centred white sprays
Mini-mum Mary Poppins	pink sprays
Mini-mum Tara	orange-yellow sprays
Mini-mum Thumbelina	quilled sprays, amber
Princess Anne (and Sport)	Reflexed, salmon-pink
Spanish Lady	Anemone-centred, claret-red, single

Cushion Koreans

There are a great number of Cushion Korean Chrysanthemums which grow quite happily in the garden and flower well during the months of August and September. There are, however, in addition, a few varieties which do not start flowering until the second or third week of October and continue in bloom until well into November. I have had Cushion Koreans in bloom as late as 15 November.

Some gardeners find it suitable to grow these chrysanthemums out of doors in a sunny warm spot, and then to dig up the Late-flowering varieties about 22 September in the north, or 15 October in the south, with a nice ball of soil to the roots. They then pot up the plants into 5-in. pots using Alex No-Soil Compost 3 as extra soil to fill the pots. Others pot the plants up into their 5-in. pots about the middle of May and then plunge these pots in the soil 15 in. apart either way. The plants thus grow on in their pots ('underground', as it were) until the end of September, when the pots are got up out of the soil. If any roots are found to have penetrated through the drainage hole at the bottom these are carefully cut off before the plants are brought into the greenhouse.

Taking the Cuttings

The cuttings of these Cushion Koreans are taken about 5 March as a rule. They strike quite easily if they are dibbled out 1 in. apart into Alex No-Soil Compost in frames or under cloches. Cover the soil with sharp silver sand ¼ in. deep, so that when the hole is made some of the sand is carried down to the point of the dibber. The bottom of the cutting should then rest on this sand. Cover the frame with its light. By 5 May the cuttings should be ready to be potted up into 3-in. pots, using John Innes Potting Compost 1 or Alex No-Soil Compost 1. Alternatively, the potting can be deferred until 15 May, when the plants can be potted up into their 5-in. pots using John Innes Compost 2 or Alex No-Soil Compost 2.

Stopping

These Cushion Chrysanthemums seldom, if ever, have to be stopped, for they break naturally – in fact they have a delightful branching habit of growth.

General Remarks

There is no need to stake the plants at all for they grow sturdily and are quite compact. They do, however, appreciate having their leaves syringed over once or twice a week in the early evening. The pots must be watered as they need it. Once the plants are in the greenhouse, they must be fed with Marinure or Farmura once a week until the flowers start to open. Once in the greenhouse or the living-room, remove the dying blooms with a pair of scissors, for this helps the plants to flower longer.

When the plants have finished flowering, the stems should be cut back to within 1 in. of soil level and the pots stood outside in the shelter of a wall or in a light shed. There they should not be allowed to dry off completely because they will be needed for producing cuttings in the spring. As each plant may be relied upon to produce five or six cuttings, it will only be necessary to save some of the plants in order to get the cuttings required for the following season.

Pests and Diseases

Koreans are seldom badly attacked by diseases or pests, but if aphids or leaf miners are seen in September the plants may be sprayed with Malathion.

Varieties

The following are perhaps the most suitable Dwarf Korean varities for growing in 5-in. pots:

Name	Description	Height	Time of Flowering
Azaleanum	Semi-double, salmon-pink	15 in.	October–November
Bonfire	Double, scarlet	18 in.	October
Glow	Semi-double, salmon-rose	15 in.	October–November
Ladybird	Double, russet-red	12 in.	October–November
October Charm	Single, rich red	18 in.	mid-October–November
Startler	bright claret-pink	15 in.	October

Pompons

A number of Dwarf Pompons flower quite rapidly out of doors in July, August and September. On the other hand, there are few varieties which can be grown as pot plants for flowering indoors in October and November. There are, of course, Pompon Chrysanthemums which can be grown to a height of 4 ft, but the gardener who is keen on growing them in 5-in. pots concentrates on varieties which grow no taller than 18 in.

Pompon Chrysanthemums are very hardy indeed and will grow in any normal soil. There is no stopping or even disbudding to do.

Propagation

The plants are propagated by means of cuttings usually taken in late February or early March. These can be struck as advised in Chapter 3. When fully rooted, the plants can be potted into 3-in. pots in John Innes Potting Compost 2 or Alex No-Soil Compost 2. A month or six weeks later they can be potted on into 5-in. pots using John Innes Potting Compost 3 or Alex No-Soil Compost 2. Some gardeners purposely delay potting up so that they can get the plants straight into their 5-in. pots and so save the time and money expended on the first potting. Firm potting is essential in all cases.

General Care

Because the plants are growing in 5-in. pots the roots are somewhat restricted, so a fair amount of water has to be given every

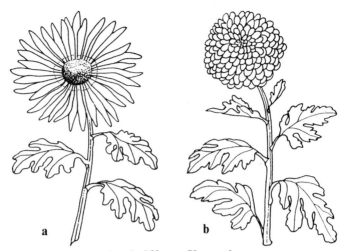

a. A typical Korean Chrysanthemum
b. A typical Dwarf Pompon Chrysanthemum

two or three days; when it comes to the middle of the summer, water them every day. Starting at the beginning of August, Marinure or Farmura can be given once a week until the plants start to flower.

The pots may be stood on ashes outside or plunged into the soil. It will not be necessary to bring them into the greenhouse until the beginning of October. Both out of doors and under glass the pots will need to be spaced out at least 18 in. apart because of their spreading growth. Remove any dead or dying blooms as they appear, cutting them off with a sharp pair of scissors.

When the plants have finished flowering, cut the stems down to soil level and store the plants as advised for Cushion Koreans.

Varieties

The following are perhaps the best early Dwarf Pompon varieties to grow for flowering in pots:

Name	Description	Height
Bronze Fairie	bronze	12 in.
Cameo	white	15 in.
Denise	yellow	12 in.
Fairie	pink	12 in.
Glow	orange	18 in.
Imp	crimson	18 in.
Purple Fairie	purple	12 in.
Salmon Fairie	salmon	12 in.

Charms

Charm Chrysanthemums are considered quite different from the other types mentioned in this chapter. The plants are invariably raised by seed sowing, which is done in boxes under glass during the months of January or February. Suttons, the Royal Seedsmen, have specialized in 'the Charms'.

For seed sowing used John Innes Seed Compost or Alex No-Soil Compost. Put this into 2-in. deep seed trays, press it down level so that it is ¼ in. lower than the top of the box. Sow the seeds very thinly over the top, press them into the soil with the wooden presser and sift a little silver sand over the top of the seeds, pressing this down lightly also. Give a light watering through the fine rose of a can and place the box or boxes on the staging of the greenhouse covered with a sheet of glass or a piece of newspaper. Remove the glass every day for wiping, and when the seedlings are through take off the glass altogether.

Grow the seedlings on at a temperature of 60 degrees F and when they are about 1 in. high, pot them up individually into 3-in. pots using John Innes Compost 1 or Alex No-Soil Compost 1. A month or six weeks later the plants should be ready to pot up into 5-in. pots. By the end of May, plants may be stood outside on ashes in an open situation. There they will be watered as they grow and by the end of September or early October, when the plants begin to show their flower buds, they may be brought into the greenhouse and put on to the staging.

The plants do quite well in a fairly cold house, it being necessary to have only a little heat to give a buoyant atmosphere. Open the ventilators on most days, only keeping them closed if it is very frosty or if there is fog about. The plants should come into flower towards the end of October and if looked after carefully may easily be encouraged to go on blooming until Christmas.

Stopping

In order to make certain that the plants break in the early stages of their life, it is a good idea to pinch out the growing points of the specimens ten days after they have been potted up into their 3-in. pots.

Varieties

A few varieties are listed on page 114. There is, also, a good colour range of star-shaped flowers which can be had by seed sowing. A double-flowering section is sold under the name of Charm *flora plena*. The seeds produce plants which bloom for quite long periods. Good specimens of these particular chrysanthemums in pots can often reach over 2 ft across. Therefore, when standing out of doors on ashes or in the greenhouse on the staging, they need more room than Pompons or Cushion Koreans.

Mini-mums   The dwarf pot chrysanthemums which may be purchased in the shops are produced under artificial lighting and temperature control. Mini-mums are the only naturally grown dwarf pot chrysanthemums and are ideally suitable for floral decoration in the home. So far Woolman's have three varieties: Tara (bronze), Mary Poppins (pink), and Thumbelina (chrome yellow). These will grow in temperatures down to about 45 degrees and can be timed, therefore, to flower at any time during the year. The length of time between potting and the first flower appearing can be as little as six weeks in the summer and about ten weeks during the winter.

Between 15 March and 15 September the plants must be blacked out until colour shows in the bud. To do this is extremely simple; it is sufficient to put a box over them at tea-time and take it off in the morning. Extra cover can be put over the box if it is not quite light-proof. Apart from occasional watering, there is little else to do.

A rooted cutting potted about the middle or the end of October will be a mass of flower for Christmas. All the varieties have long flowering periods lasting four to six weeks. After flowering they can be cut down, and later fresh cuttings can be taken in the normal way, rooted and grown into a small pot plant as before. Height varies from 6 in. to 8 in. Several other varieties will be introduced in the near future. No disbudding, stopping, or chemical control is needed. They have a musk-like scent.

Perpetuals   In addition to the types of chrysanthemums already mentioned, there are the Perpetual-flowering Chrysanthemums which were introduced by Woolman's some years ago. The plants grow from 9 to 12 in. high and produce masses of flowers 3 in. or so across.

The secret with these Perpetual-flowering Chrysanthemums is to root the cuttings in succession throughout the year. Growers who have facilities for rooting cuttings in January may pot the plants up into 3-in. pots in February and flowers will appear some time in March. Directly flowering is over the plants may be cut down. The shoots which develop from the base will produce a second lot of bloom, especially if the plants are potted up at this time into 5-in. pots, using John Innes Potting Compost 2 or Alex No-Soil Compost 2.

The cuttings taken in February should first flower in April, with the second blooming a month after the second blooming of the first cuttings. One can thus go on taking cuttings month after month from the beginning of July, and with care it is possible to have chrysanthemums in flower in pots all the year round. Generally speaking, the plants will never be taller than 1 ft and no stopping is ever necessary. The pots can be fed once a fortnight or so with diluted Marinure once the plants are growing well.

Varieties

There are only three varieties, produced by Woolman's. These are: Perpetual Pink, Perpetual Yellow and Perpetual White; the last is rather shaggy.

10 Single-flowered Chrysanthemums

How true it is to say that one man's meat is another man's poison. There are many people – women in particular, who dislike large Double Chrysanthemums and just dote on Singles. Visitors to our Demonstration Gardens will stop, maybe, at a particularly large Single and think it far more beautiful than some of the large Exhibition varieties that have been grown with such care.

The singles have been described as charming, dainty, unusual, light, fascinating, beautiful and so on. Sometimes the greatest admiration comes from people who have never realized that there are single forms of chrysanthemums. They know Oxeye daisies which are, of course, *Chrysanthemums maximums*, and because these are often dyed by market gardeners, they imagine that Single Chrysanthemums are dyed also.

Single Chrysanthemum

There are, of course, Early-flowering Singles and Late-flowering Singles, and details of available varieties are given later on. As far as culture is concerned, this hardly differs from the normal methods as described in Chapter 6 for the Earlies, and in Chapter 8 for the Lates.

Stopping and Timing

Allow the November and December varieties to break naturally, as they usually do, during the first two weeks of May. Any that have not broken by, say, 18 May should then be stopped. Occasionally there are varieties that need stopping earlier but this is the exception rather than the rule. Such varieties, Desert Song for example, are stopped or timed at the end of April.

The Early-flowering Singles should be allowed to break naturally unless the district is such a late northern one that the gardener is most anxious for the varieties to flower earlier. Many of the Earlies do not flower naturally until about the middle of September but they break naturally about the middle of June. If, however, they are stopped about 20 May, they may be encouraged to flower early in September.

93

Disbudding

A certain amount of disbudding is necessary to bring about larger blooms. It is a simple matter to pinch out, with thumb and forefinger, the tiny flower buds at the side of the main terminal flower. This can be done with the Early varieties as well as the November and December ones.

Weather

There is little doubt that the Single varieties of chrysanthemum stand wet weather better, on the whole, than Doubles. They are not so easily spotted by rain or damaged by wind. The rain drops seem to pour off the Single petals easily and are not held in the flowers, as so often happens in the case of Doubles.

Frost seldom damages Singles – they seem to be far hardier. I would therefore recommend them for gardens regarded as 'frost pockets'. The flowers, being daintier, do not provide such resistance to wind, and it is therefore sensible to grow Singles in gardens that tend to be wind-swept. Generally speaking, Singles are easier to grow than Doubles, and they can be planted, manured and looked after in a similar manner to their larger, more pompous Double cousins.

Varieties

Name	Description	Spray* or Disbud	Height
GOOD EARLY-FLOWERING VARIETIES			
Caradoc	bright yellow	disbud	2½ ft
Curlew	bright rose	spray	3 ft
Doreen Woolman	golden orange	disbud	4 ft
Firebrand	terracotta	disbud	3 ft
Jean	rosy bronze	disbud	2¼ ft
Kitty	rose-pink, white zone, very large	disbud	2½ ft
Major Robertson	scarlet	disbud	2½ ft
Nectar	almond blossom pink	spray	3 ft
September Gem	yellow	spray	2½ ft
Shirley Crimson	deep crimson, yellow disc	spray	2 ft
Singlemoon	orange-bronze, green centre	disbud	3 ft
Singlesun	golden, green centre	disbud	3 ft
Yellow Charm	bright yellow	spray	3 ft

* The term 'spray' indicates that the plant should be allowed to grow naturally.

GOOD LATE-FLOWERING VARIETIES

Albert Cooper	large yellow	disbud	4½ ft
Alice Fitton	rosy purple	disbud or spray	3½ ft
Alliance	terracotta	disbud	4 ft
Broadacre	perfect white	disbud	3 ft
Chesswood Beauty	crimson	disbud or spray	4 ft
Crimson Crown	crimson with yellow ring	disbud	4 ft
Desert Song	chestnut	disbud	3 ft
Edwin Painter	golden yellow	disbud or spray	3½ ft
Midlander	bronze	disbud	4 ft
Red Woolman's Glory	red	disbud	4 ft
Sybil	apricot	disbud or spray	3½ ft
Sylphide	pink	disbud	4 ft
Woolman's Glory	chestnut	disbud	4 ft

11 Large 'Japs'

Gardeners still refer to the Large Exhibition Chrysanthemums as 'Japs' even though the name has been officially dropped for some time now. The reason, of course, why the designation 'Japanese' has been dropped is that the great bulk of the modern varieties are British through and through, and do not come from the East at all.

Propagation

The cuttings are struck as advised in Chapter 3, but as early as possible, some of them, in fact, during the month of December. The varieties that are slower in growth and have the largest number of petals within their flowers need to be rooted earlier. Second crown varieties invariably need rooting in December or January. With a variety in the Majestic group, a group with large numbers of petals, try and get the rooting done in September. If, on the other hand, a variety has far fewer petals, Golden Trueman for instance, then it is sufficient to get the cuttings struck at the end of February.

After the cuttings stage, the plants are potted up into 3-in. pots using John Innes Compost 2 or Alex No-Soil Compost 2. They then grow on for a month or six weeks in these pots, either on the staging of a greenhouse at a temperature of 45 or 50 degrees F, or in a deep cold frame. They should then be ready to be potted up into 5-in. pots using John Innes Compost 3 or Alex No-Soil Compost 3. This potting must be firmer than the first.

From these 5-in. pots the plants go on into 9-in. pots, when John Innes Compost 4 or Alex No-Soil Compost 4 is used. This time the potting must be very firmly done. A 2-in. space must be left between the firmed compost and the top of the pot. This enables the gardener to add a little more compost as a top dressing, first on 7 July, then on 30 July, then again on 20 August and yet again about 20 September. A $\frac{1}{4}$-in. layer of Potting Compost 4 is usually applied on each occasion. It helps to bring the white feeding roots upwards.

Red Desert Song, a Single-flowered variety

96

Stopping and Timing

When growing Large Exhibition varieties it is as well (as a beginner) to follow almost slavishly the instructions given in the catalogues of the firms from which the plants are bought. Some varieties, like Charles Shoesmith, break naturally; others, like Margaret Shoesmith, must be stopped by 15 April to flower on the first crown. Beryl Shirley is flowered on the natural second bud, while Stately is not stopped until the end of June. The purpose is to have the flowers in for show early in November. Many of the Incurved Exhibition kinds are flowered on the second crowns, the first stop being made, say, in early April and the second stop in about the last week of June. This is how I treat varieties like Audrey Shoesmith, Leslie Tandy and Arona.

General Care

The plants should be grown outside from about 20 May in the south and early in June in the north. The pots are stood on the typical ash standing ground, as advised in Chapter 8, the tall bamboos being tied firmly to the wires above so that the pots cannot blow over. During the summer period, the pots must be watered regularly and a sharp look-out kept for pests and diseases. Spray with Malathion for pests, and Karathane in the case of mildew.

Instead of waiting until the end of September or early October before bringing the plants into the greenhouse, it is usual to start the housing on 15 September. Arrange the plants so that the taller ones are at the back and the dwarf ones towards the front, and give each chrysanthemum sufficient room to breathe. Always get in as many pots as possible but don't allow the leaves of one plant to touch the leaves of the next, or fungus troubles like botrytis or mildew may occur.

A few days after housing, fumigate the greenhouse with two appropriate 'smokes', one for pests and another for fungus diseases.

Whatever you do, don't coddle the plants. For the first three weeks, at any rate, open the ventilators night and day. After that, ventilate in the day-time and close down in the late afternoon. If it should prove to be particularly sunny early in October, protect the plants against the sun rays by spraying a little 'Summer Cloud' on the glass or by pinning some Rokolene material on the outside of the bars of the greenhouse.

Dolliette, an unusual Korean variety

About 10 October be prepared to heat the greenhouse a little so as to create a buoyant atmosphere. The plants certainly do not like high temperatures but equally they dislike damp conditions. Some gardeners use a heating element with a fan, by which warm air may be blown through the greenhouse, and this is ideal for preventing the damping off of the petals of the blooms. It is possible to use this heater in conjunction with a thermostat, to make sure that the temperature never rises above the desired level of 50 degrees F or so.

Take or secure the bud you wish to flower by removing the other little buds or side shoots on the stems. Always start disbudding from the top of the stem downwards and do this when the buds or shoots are long enough to be broken off sideways, i.e. when they are ½ in. long. Be careful not to damage the leaves of the plants when the unwanted buds and shoots are removed. Just leave the terminal flower bud at the end of each stem.

An Incurved
Chrysanthemum

The plants are usually fed about once every ten days with Marinure until such time as the flower bud starts to open.

Varieties

The following varieties of Large and Medium Exhibition Chrysanthemums may be recommended:

Name	Description	Height	Stopping or Natural Break	1st or 2nd Crown
Amethyst	purple	4 ft	N.B.	1st
Bill Bye	rich golden yellow	3 ft	N.B.	1st
Birmingham	crimson	4 ft	N.B.	1st
Cossack	crimson	4 ft	N.B. twice	2nd
Duke of Kent	white	3½ ft	N.B.	1st
Gigantic	chestnut	4 ft	1st week May	1st
Green Goddess	sea-green	4½ ft	N.B.	1st
Harry Gee	silvery pink	3½ ft	N.B.	1st
Jessie Habgood	white	3 ft	1st week May	1st
Mark Woolman	yellow	4½ ft	2nd week April	1st
Shirley Primrose	yellow	4½ ft	mid-March and mid-May	2nd
Yellow Duke	yellow	3½ ft	N.B.	1st
Winn Quinn	yellow	4 ft	N.B.	1st

12 Showing Chrysanthemums

Some readers will probably skip this chapter, saying quite firmly that they are not going to exhibit chrysanthemums in a Show. They merely want to grow the flowers to create a beautiful garden and to decorate the house. There is little doubt, however, that many readers, once they have been 'bitten by the chrysanthemum bug', will later on gladly return to this chapter, determined 'to have a go'.

The first step in the right direction is to join The National Chrysanthemum Society, whose General Secretary is Mr S. G. Gosling, 65 St Margaret's Avenue, Whetstone, London N20. It will then be possible to obtain a copy of the *Chrysanthemum Manual*, first published in October 1957. This manual has a special section for exhibitors. After reading this, go to one of the Shows run by The National Chrysanthemum Society and see what other people are doing.

The man who intends to grow for Show naturally takes far more care of his blooms than the one who is just growing for the needs of his own house. Earwigs may mark a chrysanthemum bloom in a night. The marks may not unduly depress a home producer, but to the exhibitor such marks can make the difference between a first prize and no prize at all. The exhibitor, therefore, has to take infinite care of his plants. He must know the correct use of insecticides and fungicides and, in fact, be prepared to prevent rather than cure.

It isn't necessarily the enormous blooms that win the prizes. Huge blooms are sometimes coarse. Judges at Shows may easily prefer more moderately-sized blooms which are perfect in shape and colour and absolutely fresh also. Don't try and exhibit flowers that are 'past it' – the blooms should be coming to perfection so that by the time they are judged they are perfect.

Remember that a judge is human. He has been an exhibitor himself and he knows all the tricks of the trade. He looks underneath the blooms to see whether there are petals that have passed their best. He looks into the middle of a bloom to see (in the case of the true doubles) whether there is any sign of an eye at all. The exhibitor, therefore, must go over all the flowers very carefully, gently picking off injured or brown petals with a pair of forceps, and rejecting Double flowers that have any sign of an eye at all.

It is best to leave the blooms on the plants until two days before they are needed. With varieties that do not seem to take up water easily, be sure to crush the base of the stems with a pair of pliers so that the water can enter. Always cut, bruise, and put the stems in water as soon as possible. Never cut the stems out of doors and then leave them out of water for half an hour or more. When this is done it is possible that an airlock will occur, preventing the water from rising up the stems as it should.

Exhibitors who have to go to Shows some distance away may have to cut their blooms four days before the event, and to ensure that they are in the right condition they put them into deep water in a cool place. In these circumstances it helps to put a little salt in the water, using a teaspoonful to a pint and a half.

When putting chrysanthemum stems in water, remove some of the bottom leaves or else these may absorb much of the moisture which ought to rise up and reach the flower. Don't over-defoliate, however, for the stems must have some leaves on them when the blooms are put in for a Show. The best room or shed in which to place the chrysanthemums in water is one where the light is partially shaded and the atmosphere dry. Always cut more flowers than are actually needed for the exhibit so that on the day of the display there is plenty of choice for the final six, eight or twelve blooms needed.

Remember that when you are asked to put up a vase of blooms, each flower must be of the same size, the same shape and the same colour shade. Also, the stems should be of the same length. In fact, all the flowers should be as nearly identical as possible. Be sure to cut on the same day all the blooms that are to be shown in one particular class. The judges, with their expert knowledge, can easily detect blooms that have been cut two or three days before others.

Dressage

In the early days of Chrysanthemum Shows, gardeners would spend hours with the huge Jap blooms rolling and curling the petals, or whatever might be necessary to make certain that the great ball of bloom was perfect. Fortunately, today most modern varieties are perfect and so there is hardly any titivation to do. There may easily be an odd petal to be pulled out or another petal that has to be slightly adjusted, but that is all. Perhaps it is the Incurved varieties that give the greatest trouble. The man who wins prizes puts up his flowers perfectly formed. This means that he may have to tweak out one or two of the centre petals even as the flower is opening, so that the outer petals can curve in properly and thus produce the beautiful globe.

Studying the Schedule

It would seem quite unnecessary to remind prospective exhibitors of the great importance of studying the schedule carefully. I have judged at many Shows, however, and it is most embarrassing to have to disqualify an excellent exhibit because the schedule categorically stated six blooms and only five were entered. Sometimes mistakes are made concerning the type of chrysanthemum. If the schedule says 'Incurved Decoratives' it means Incurved Decoratives and not Reflexed Decoratives.

Don't make the mistake of saying 'I didn't know' or 'I didn't understand', for it is a simple matter, in the case of a local Show, to see a member of the Committee or, in the case of a National Show, to discuss the point over the telephone with the Secretary, who will be only too glad to explain the whole thing to you. Please don't, however, worry a Secretary the day before the Show as he will be far too busy to talk to you. It is even possible, when staging an exhibit, to ask a question of a committee member. It would be far better, even at this late stage, to make enquiries than to make mistakes.

Practice Makes Perfect

If you intend to compete in, say, 1976 it is a very good idea to go round the Show in 1975 and make notes. You can see which varieties have won in each class, which have come second and which are 'also rans'. You can practise being a judge yourself, and try to discover for yourself why the decisions have been made. Note the size of the blooms in each class, the length of the stems and so on, and if the Show is not a large one, it may be possible to get an introduction to some of the winners in order to discuss the exhibits with them.

It is always possible to practise staging at home. For this purpose, of course, don't use the blooms that are going to be put in the Show but others that are similar in size and shape. You will then learn how to display flowers so that they look at their best; some with taller stems at the back and others with shorter stems at the front, for instance.

At the previous year's Show make notes as to how the blooms have been arranged in each class, and obtain information from the Secretary as to whether you are allowed to provide your own vases or whether you must use those belonging to the Society. In cases where you provide the vases, see to it that these are bought of the right height, size and shape. Do this well in advance so that you can practise staging in the actual vases. Always have one or two vases left over as spares in case of breakages.

Courtesy
It sometimes happens that an exhibitor enters a class with every intention of putting in an exhibit of, say, six vases. Unfortunately, when the time comes the gardener may find that the flowers are not in a fit condition to show, and he is therefore obliged to cancel. Please don't just groan! Take the precaution of ringing up the Secretary immediately, or writing to him, to let him know that you cannot fulfil your entry. He will then be able to adjust the spacing on the tables at the Show.

Necessary Preparation
There is a type of exhibitor who will leave the entering up of cards, and the like, until the day of the Show itself; he may even be seen making out his cards when the flowers are in their vases. It is far better, of course, to get all cards entered up a week or so beforehand and to see that these are right with the schedule. Note carefully from the schedule how many vases will be needed and so prepare them and get them packed ready to take. As you become an experienced exhibitor you will learn to have a small attaché case containing a knife, secateurs, green string, tweezers, a camelhair brush, a biro pen, a notebook, some spare wire and so on. It is convenient, also, to have a small Hawes watering-can so that the vases can be topped up with water if necessary. Most people take a bucket along with them as well, because one cannot rely on the Show providing enough buckets for every exhibitor.

At the Show
The exhibitor will have taken a great deal of trouble to ensure that he has everything he needs. He will have cut spare blooms

of the various varieties so that if there are accidents he will not have to suffer the indignity of having to 'borrow' from somebody else. The blooms will have been carefully packed in deep boxes so that they cannot move about, with special pads, made of wood with paper around them, on which to rest the necks of the blooms. The chrysanthemums will thus have arrived at the Show undamaged.

Get to the Show early so that you have plenty of time for staging. The Committee will willingly let you know when you may arrive – generally speaking, the earlier the better. Carry the boxes to the Show very carefully, and the moment you arrive get them under cover where it is cool, preferably in a dark and quiet corner. Avoid leaving them out in the sun or rain.

Show a friendly spirit and give a hand, if need be, to another exhibitor with his boxes; he will be willing to give you a helping hand later on. Fill your bucket or buckets with water and put the stems of the chrysanthemums into the containers as soon as possible, to give them a really good drink.

Next fill up the vases, put them in position according to schedule and see that they are in the exact spot allotted to your exhibit. Start arranging the flowers in the back row first and then the front row and, if necessary, move them to change the position of the varieties if you are not satisfied with the first effort.

Don't be tempted to waste time watching other exhibitors. Go on quietly with your own work. Don't be flustered, even if the blooms in the Exhibition hall or tent seem far smaller than they did when you had them at home. Look at the flowers carefully and if any dust has fallen on them during the journey, remove this carefully with a camelhair brush. If any of the florets are out of place, re-arrange them with a pair of tweezers. It is usually permissible to push down some moss into the vases in between the stems, to make certain that the blooms keep their positions.

If you have finished staging nice and early, and there is plenty of time before the judging, it may be possible, and advisable, to cover the blooms with a sheet or two of white tissue paper, to protect them until the bell goes and you are called out of the tent or room.

Don't forget to ask for the correct exhibitor's card. This has to be put face downwards in front of the exhibit. Make certain, if you are entering a number of classes, to put the right card in position.

Ten minutes before judging time, or at least before the bell goes, make certain that all your exhibits are exactly right. It isn't difficult to enter three white Decoratives in the class which asks for five white Decoratives, and vice versa. If you have unfortunately put both exhibits upon the wrong table, it shouldn't take you a minute to change them over. If you have made a mistake, check up with the Secretary who can usually help by making some alterations.

Once the flowers have been staged, and the judges are doing their work, leave the Show, have a meal or a drink, and don't come back again until all the judging has been completed. It is very nerve-racking to stand about at the entrance of a marquee or hall, and judges do not like to see impatient exhibitors. Don't be tempted to ask a steward friend to come and let you know of a win, early on, for stewards can sometimes make a mistake, and anyway it's unfair to ask officials to help in this way.

A Special Note for Beginners

Concentrate on one or two classes and go in for these with great enthusiasm. Don't dissipate your strength trying to enter too many classes at one go. The judge is always said to be looking for the five S's, i.e. Solidity, Substance, Symmetry, Smoothness and Soundness, but he undoubtedly looks for the three F's as well, Finish, Floret colour and Freshness. He won't think size all-important.

Growing for Show

People who have been to Chrysanthemum Shows, and made a note of the perfect blooms exhibited, sometimes come and ask me what is the great secret, as they call it. There is no one great secret in producing perfect chrysanthemums, it's just a question of taking the greatest pains right from the beginning of the plant's career. The cutting must be a good one, taken from a stool that has been warm-water treated so that there is no eelworm present. Care should be taken so that the cutting roots within five weeks, and is then allowed to grow on without any check, first of all in its 3-in. pot, and then in its 5-in. pot, and lastly, if it's an Early out-of-doors and if it's a Late, in its 9- or 10-in. pot.

The stopping or timing will be done in accordance with the instructions given or as the result of experience. The number of branches will be reduced to four if the variety tends to be weak and to six if it is strong. When disbudding, all the side buds will be left until they are $\frac{1}{4}$ in. long. White and yellow varieties may need a length of butter muslin held over them a week or two before the Show, and I have known northern growers to use Dutch Lights as umbrellas over the blooms of outdoor varieties.

Flood the ground or the pots with water the night before packing the blooms and sever the stems as early in the morning as possible. Then, having bruised them or dipped the bottom inch of stem in hot water for five seconds, put the stems in a deep bucket of water for at least twelve hours before packing. After cutting white blooms, it may be advisable to spray the flowers with really clean water and then shake the excess water off afterwards, very carefully.

With Singles grown in pots for exhibition, it is often necessary to do the second stopping of the stronger varieties during the first week of June, and the weaker or medium varieties about the third week of June. Three good breaks should be allowed on each stem, to produce six good blooms per plant.

From mid-June the pot plants will need feeding once a fortnight with Marinure or Farmura. Feeding continues until the flowers are half open; by then the pots are in the greenhouse and growing at a temperature of 55 degrees F.

In the case of Singles, most judges prefer an absolutely flat flower. Florets that are slightly incurving are not admired.

With Large Exhibition Chrysanthemums, get the cuttings struck at the end of December, pot them up four weeks later into 3-in. pots using John Innes Compost 1 or Alex No-Soil Compost 1. Pot on about 20 March into 5-in. pots using John Innes Compost 3 or Alex No-Soil Compost 2, and pot on again into 9- or 10-in. pots about 20 May, using John Innes Compost 4 or Alex No-Soil Compost 3. Stop about 10 June and concentrate on the three best side growths, allowing these to grow until the buds are seen at the top, when disbudding should be done. In the case of varieties which are to be grown on the second crown bud, stop again, allowing only one stem to develop on each branch. Keep to three stems per plant, whether on the first or second crown.

Adding Sweetness
Successful exhibitors insist that there is a lot to be said for giving chrysanthemums some sugar after the blooms have been cut. Some add two Dextrose tablets to the bucket of water in which the blooms are placed, others even use them, I believe, in the vases at the Show. The purpose is to increase the freshness and bright colour of the flowers. Other exhibitors, who won't use Dextrose, adopt this formula: eight large teaspoonfuls of granu-

lated sugar, one teaspoonful of powdered alum and one tea-spoonful of Milton. The three are mixed and added to one gallon of water. (The only reason Milton is used is that it is a dis-infectant and so stops the growth of bacteria.)

If colour intensity can be improved after the blooms are cut, then it is necessary, as has already been mentioned earlier, to re-move some of the lower leaves before the stems are stood deeply in water.

I should say that I myself have not actually used either Dex-trose or sugar, but I am passing on the information because others swear by their use.

13 Electric Light and Flowering Time

Some years ago I carried out a number of experiments in connection with the use of electric light for growing chrysanthemums at night-time. Most garden plants in the world can be classified into two big groups, those that like long days and those that like long nights (or 'short hours'). In other words, some plants, if they are to do their best, prefer to grow in the summer-time when there are many hours of sunshine, while other groups of plants, on the other hand, do best in the winter-time when the hours of sunshine are reduced.

Even within one group of plants it is possible to have varieties that do better on long days and others that do well when there are long nights; some varieties of lettuce, like Cheshunt Early Giant, for instance, are perfectly happy to grow in a cool greenhouse during the winter, while others, like Newmarket, prefer to grow out of doors in the summer. In addition, there are groups of plants which are classed as being 'indifferent' to lengths of day or night.

A few years ago it would have been said, categorically, that the chrysanthemum was a short-day plant because it invariably needs fourteen complete hours of darkness in each twenty-four hours if it is to produce the correct proportion of flower buds, and cause them to open properly. Latterly, experiments and demonstrations have shown that it isn't right to be dogmatic in this respect. There are types and varieties which are the exception rather than the rule.

Almost all the chrysanthemum varieties which come under the section Decoratives and which normally flower in the greenhouse during the months of November and December, are indeed 'short day' types. As against this, there are, of course, large numbers of Early-flowering varieties which flower quite happily during the summer-time when the days are long. Mention has been made in Chapter 9 of the Perpetual-flowering Chrysanthemums which can certainly be expected to flower

107

every month in the year. These don't seem to mind whether the days are long or short. The third big exception is the November-flowering group of Large Exhibition varieties. These are definitely 'long day' kinds because they start to produce their flower buds towards the end of July and the beginning of August when the garden has almost the maximum length of sunlight.

Having said this, it should still be made clear that a gardener – be he the veriest amateur – can do something by means of electric light to alter the flowering period of a certain number or, maybe, a large number of the varieties he grows. The method adopted is the simple one of stringing a number of electric light bulbs a foot above the chrysanthemums exactly where they are growing out of doors, and then arranging a time-switch so that the plants are illuminated for about two hours in the middle of the night. It could be arranged, for instance, that the electric light was switched on at midnight and switched off at 2 a.m. As a result the plants would not have the normal short day and so flowering would be deferred.

This system of altering the date of flowering is called Photo-periodism. Some gardeners have managed to save expense by having special time-switches which turn the light on for not more than two seconds every two minutes. By interrupting the normal fourteen to sixteen hours of darkness in this way the plants may be forced to flower later. It is only necessary, therefore, to interrupt the long night just a little for later flowering to be achieved.

If readers are particularly interested in this phase of the work, I would advise them to read *Chrysanthemums the Year Round* by Searle and Machin. Far greater use could be made of electric light. There are definite indications, for instance, that if the chrysanthemum stools are given more light during the months of January and February, more and better chrysanthemum cuttings would be produced.

It seems sensible, even in a beginner's book, to mention the possibilities of Photo-periodism. There will probably be some readers who will be so keen on the whole idea that they will do their own research, and so benefit other chrysanthemum growers.

14 Chrysanthemums All the Year Round

It was as far back as 1921 that work was first being done on chrysanthemums that would flower month after month. It wasn't until after 1950, however, that information started drifting through from the USA about the methods that might be adopted to produce cut-flower chrysanthemums all the year round.

Certain firms, particularly in the south of England, concentrated on this then unusual method of chrysanthemum production, and before long it was found possible to have chrysanthemums not only as cut flowers but also as flowering plants in pots all the year round. At one time it was thought that this would result in the chrysanthemum becoming unpopular, but interestingly enough the opposite has been the case. Precision growing, as it is called, has after all resulted in better quality and cleaner blooms.

It is unlikely that beginners will want to devote their greenhouse or greenhouses to the production of chrysanthemums only, but those who are keen enough on this flower to do this will probably divide up the floor space of the greenhouse, so that they can plant up a new section every six or seven weeks. The flowers will then turn in ready for cutting nearly every month of the year.

It must be borne in mind, however, that despite the special production of rooted cuttings there is a difference in the time needed to get a particular section into flower. You may need a maximum of nineteen weeks in the middle of winter, whereas it isn't difficult to get chrysanthemum plants to flower within twelve weeks in the middle of summer.

To succeed with this work it is necessary to buy in the struck cuttings to plant at a particular time. For October flowering, for instance, the planting is usually done in June, and for November flowering, in July. Messrs Framptons of Leythorne, Chichester, issue an excellent directive on the subject.

Gardeners who don't want to divide the soil area of the greenhouse into eight could perhaps divide it into three. In this case it will be possible to buy rooted cuttings for planting in August for the first area so that there will be plenty of plants for Christmas. The second area could then be planted early in January, to give chrysanthemums at the end of April, and the third area, planted with struck cuttings early in May, would then supply chrysanthemums during the month of August.

There is a different schedule for the growing of spray chrysanthemums – not everyone bothers to disbud chrysanthemums; some people much prefer a spray of flowers to a single bloom. In the case of varieties that are going to be grown for spray, the amateur may like to divide his greenhouse space into three and then obtain young plants from the nurserymen early in July for the first area. He will then get flowers during the month of October. Then, if the second area is planted late in October, there will be a supply of spray chrysanthemums during the month of March. The third planting will be done about 20 March, for flowering from about the middle of June to the end of July.

The information in Chapter 13, on the use of electric light at flowering time, should be referred to. Remember that it will be necessary to use electric light for the plants you wish to have in flower during the winter-time. You may, however, need blackout material for putting over the plants that you intend to flower from about the beginning of August to the middle of October.

I am particularly fond of the varieties which, delayed by the use of electric light, flower for Christmas. The varieties used have to be fast-growing kinds and ones which will produce high-quality blooms as late as six weeks after their natural flowering dates. Generally speaking, these are the fast-growing varieties which the chrysanthemum expert says normally have an eleven-week response. Varieties I have in mind for this purpose include Mefo, Woking Scarlet, Fred Shoesmith, Parade and Blaze.

It makes a great deal of difference, of course, where the chrysanthemums are grown. It is useful, for instance, for the area to have a southern aspect and, as has been suggested in two previous chapters, growing plants must always have protection from strong winds. The greenhouse itself should be as light as possible inside. The woodwork must be painted so that it is a really shiny white, the walls must be white-washed too, as well as the paths and hot-water pipes. Everything must be done to see that the plants get the maximum reflected light. This cannot be over-emphasized. For the plants that are growing in winter-time, the temperature in the greenhouse should be 60 degrees F night and day. It is most important to keep this minimum night temperature correct. If the temperature drops there may be a delay in the flowering time.

It is only when the flower buds are actually visible that a reduction in temperature can be started. My own plan is to try and drop down to 58 degrees F by the end of the first week, and to 56 degrees F at the end of the second week. A temperature of 52 degrees F should be reached for the flowering period.

Don't start to go in for this fascinating method of growing chrysanthemums until a letter has been sent to a firm like Woolman's Nurseries. They will be able to recommend the right varieties under the particular conditions concerned.

I use 100-watt lamps spaced 6 ft apart, 4 ft above the chrysanthemum bed. During the months of April, May, August and September the automatic switch turns on the electricity for two hours, i.e. from midnight to 2 a.m.; in October and March, the electric light goes on from midnight to 3 a.m.; in November and February, from 11 p.m. to 3 a.m., and during December and January the period is increased to five hours.

Then, to make the days artificially short, cover the whole bed of chrysanthemums from 6 to 7 p.m. with black plastic sheeting. The darkening is usually done from about 15 March until 20 September.

At the time of writing the cost of the electric cable, lamp holders and the posts used to cover a 4-ft bed, 100 ft long, is about £10 but, of course, to this figure must be added the cost of the time-switch. It is a regular bind to have to hang about from midnight to 2 or 3 o'clock in the morning to turn the electric light on and off. The electric time-switch, therefore, is of great value.

For fuller and more detailed information on this subject, read *Chrysanthemums the Year Round*, by Searle and Machin.

15 Charm, Korean and Cascade Chrysanthemums

Charms

Charm Chrysanthemums have already been referred to in Chapter 9, which dealt with Decorative dwarf pot plants. Charms, however, can be grown out-of-doors, they needn't be pot plants only. They are a relatively new race of chrysanthemums which come into full flower in eight months or so, and Messrs Suttons of Reading have made a speciality of them. I myself have had fully grown specimens just over 3 ft across and yet only 18 to 19 in. high. Such specimens are literally covered with masses of small single flowers, very much like those of the Michaelmas Daisy. The great thing about the Charm Chrysanthemum is that it grows bushy without any stopping. The leaves are finely cut and so are seldom attacked by leaf miner. The flowers may be brown, yellow, crimson, rose-pink or even blush-pink.

Seed Sowing
The seed is normally sown in February in boxes containing Alex No-Soil Compost. This should be pressed down with a wooden presser so that the top is level, and after the seeds are sown thinly over the top, not more than ⅛ in. of the compost should be sifted over in order to bury the seeds. Press this down lightly and then give a watering through the fine rose of a can. Stand the boxes on the staging of the greenhouse at a temperature of about 50 degrees F, each box being covered with a sheet of glass and a sheet of brown paper.

Once a day the glass should be removed for wiping and then put back again. The day will come when the seedlings are through and then the glass and paper can be removed altogether. When the seedlings are about 1 in. high they can be potted up into 3-in. pots using Alex No-Soil Compost 1. A fortnight or three weeks later the growing points of the plants may be pinched out to just above the fourth leaf. This encourages the plants to bush out early in their lives. Three weeks later the

A Korean Chrysanthemum

plants should be transferred to 5-in. pots using Alex No-Soil Compost 2 and a week after potting the plants may be put out into a frame for hardening off. By the end of May, it should be possible to knock the plants out of their pots and plant them in groups or drifts in a sunny border.

It is possible to buy the rooted cuttings of Charms from Woolman's Nurseries, and a list of varieties will be found below. As a rule, there is a wastage from plants raised from seed.

If you wish to grow the plants under glass or in the house it will be necessary, of course, to pot up once again, in June, into 8- or 9-in. pots. These pots will have to be placed outside on an ash base until the time comes, early in October, to bring them into the greenhouse. I have found it possible to have plants flowering in a cold house, but it is worth giving some heat in late November or early December in order to retain a buoyant atmosphere. It is advisable to ventilate well, whenever the weather permits.

Feeding

As this chrysanthemum is a gross feeder, top dressing is necessary to get the finest results. When the pots have become filled with roots, which is usually four weeks after the final potting, a weekly feed helps. Use Marinure or a good fish fertilizer for the purpose. Feeding must stop about the middle of September. Careful watch should be kept for the usual chrysanthemum pests, and spraying with nicotine or derris carried out as necessary.

Smaller Plant Varieties

There are few named varieties, but Suttons produces a pretty range of colours which grow no higher than 2ft. The few varieties that are available can also be obtained from Woolman's.

Name	Description
Apricot Charm	pretty apricot
Bullfinch	deep crimson, flowering well into December
Kingfisher	red with a touch of violet
Morning Star	clear yellow with lime green
Redbreast	red
Ringdove	pink with a circle of white at the centre
Seagull	pure white
Tang	rich tangerine

Smaller but equally attractive plants can be obtained by

sowing seed up to the middle of April in a cold frame or greenhouse. When large enough the seedlings should be pricked off into 3-in. pots, with a final potting into the 5-in. size. It will be found advantageous to plunge the pots in ashes up to the rim to help conserve moisture and thus avoid continuous watering. This method will produce well-furnished plants which will flower at about the same time as larger specimens.

Koreans

Koreans were introduced into this country from the USA. A Mr Harland P. Kelsey went to North Korea in late 1920 and early 1921 and made a large collection of chrysanthemums. These he took back to the United States with him, and then carried out a good deal of crossing with the best free-flowering varieties. We have today, therefore, what may be termed Korean Hybrids which will put up with almost any frost; most of them flower magnificently in the autumn. Unlike the other kinds of chrysanthemum which have been described in this book, it is possible to leave the roots of Korean Chrysanthemums outside the whole of the winter.

Cuttings and Division

The cuttings of these chrysanthemums may be taken as late as March and can be dibbled out in sandy compost in frames or under Ganwicks. The roots are produced quickly and easily and the plants are invariably ready to put out into the open about the middle of May. Gardeners who have no frames or Access frames will find it convenient to dig up the clumps in late April, divide them carefully into portions, and plant these portions out where they are to grow.

Culture

The little plants invariably produce their first flower buds about 1 ft from soil level and it is after this that the lateral growths develop. I have seldom had to do any stopping at all. The stems are very wiry and strong, and some varieties grow to a height of 18 in., others to a height of $2\frac{1}{2}$ ft. Perhaps the great advantage of Koreans is that they can be allowed to grow quite naturally, without any securing of buds or disbudding at all.

Varieties

The following varieties are well worth growing:

A Spoon-tipped Korean Chrysanthemum

Name	Single or Double	Description	Height	Time of Flowering
SHORTER VARIETIES				
Ada Miles	single	cream	18 in.	August
Amber Glory	double	bronze yellow	18 in.	November
Annette	semi-double	white	18 in.	October
Autumn	single	red	15 in.	November
Blush	single	pale salmon-blush	18 in.	November
Bonfire	double	crimson-scarlet	18 in.	October
Brightness	double	crimson-red	2 ft	September–October
Bronze Tench	single	yellow	18 in.	November
Carlene	double	brilliant orange	2 ft	August
Copper Nob	double	burnished copper	2 ft	August
Cream Tench	double	cream	18 in.	October–November
Crimson Tench	double	red	15 in.	October–November
Don Raynor	single	pink	2 ft	November
Dora Joice	single	crimson	2 ft	October–November
Fairy Rose	single	bright rose	18 in.	November
Falgate	double	light bronze	18 in.	October
Gloria	double	silver-pink, salmon centre	18 in.	September
Herald	single	red-bronze	15 in.	October–November
Honey Pot	single	honey-yellow	2 ft	September
Ivy Joice	single	lavender	15 in.	October–November
Janice Bailey	single	rosy pink	18 in.	October–November
Lemon Tench	single	lemon	12 in.	October–November
Little Muffet	single	strawberry-pink	18 in.	August
Lustre	double	old rose with dark centre	2 ft	September
Margery Daw	single	strawberry-red	18 in.	September
Mulberry	single	mulberry-red	15 in.	October–November
Otley Beauty	double	bright orange	18 in.	September
Otley Beauty	double	red	15 in.	October–November
Polly Flanders	single	Mandarin-red	18 in.	September
Red Joy	single	bright red	18 in.	October–November
Red Riding Hood	single	terracotta	18 in.	September
Ruby Raynor	double	golden	2 ft	October–November
Susan	single	brick-red	18 in.	August
Tawny Owl	double	yellow-tipped, deep red	1 ft	September

TALLER VARIETIES

Name	Type	Colour	Height	Month
Anne	double	white with deeper centre	2½ft	October
Brenda	single	pale mauve	2½ft	August
Canary Wonder	double	primrose-yellow	3ft	October
Cardinal	semi-double	blood-crimson	2½ft	September
Charles Nye	double	golden bronzy yellow	3½ft	October
Coral Mist	single	deep coral-pink	2½ft	September
Coral Pink	single	pyrethrum-pink	2½ft	September
Doris	semi-double	bright mauve-pink	2½ft	September
Ember Day	double	cerise-pink	2½ft	September
Flame	single	brick-red	3ft	October
Fred Rockwell	double	brilliant flame-red	2½ft	September
Golden Arrow	single	chrome-yellow	3ft	October
Hazel	single	fine apricot	2½ft	September
Leonora	double	shrimp and azalea-pink	2½ft	September
Mabel	single	cardinal red	2½ft	September
Maize Yellow	double	maize-shot pink	3ft	October
Marie	single	salmon pink	2½ft	September
Royal Command	single	rich wine purple	3ft	September
St George's Day	double	crimson red	3½ft	October
Tangerine	single	tangerine	3ft	October
Tapestry Red	double	crimson red	2½ft	September
Trafalgar Day	double	vivid magenta	3ft	October
Wedding Sunshine	double (spray single)	canary yellow	3ft	October

General Remarks

Manure and feed the land as advised for ordinary chrysan-themums because Koreans are rather greedy. Be prepared to stake the taller varieties with a bamboo – the smaller kinds will usually stand up quite stiffly without any support at all. The taller varieties will need planting about 2ft apart, but smaller kinds may go in as close as 18in. square, and if planted in this way they produce a perfect mass of bloom which completely hides the soil.

Koreans are ideal plants for cutting. The stem can be cut low down, so that there is a magnificent display to bring into the house, looking most natural in a vase, or, if preferred, the individual branches may be cut, the stems being quite long enough for modern vases.

Cascades   Cascade Chrysanthemums were first introduced in 1933 and soon afterwards I saw them growing very successfully in the greenhouses at Windsor Castle. Since that time they have been much used for flowering displays in Buckingham Palace.

The Cascade Chrysanthemum is really a free-flowering small-flowered type which can easily be raised from seed. The plants come into flower about the end of October and continue right through to Christmas and beyond. The colours range from white to pale pink and rose pink, and there are also shades of yellow, bronze, red and crimson. Many of the flowers are delicately scented and some of them prove most useful for cutting.

The plants can be grown in all kinds of curious ways: in umbrella and fan shapes, and as pillars or large bushes. It is possible to grow the plants as standards and weeping standards and, of course, to train them so that they cascade down from the top like a waterfall.

Seed Sowing

Sow the seed in John Innes Seed Compost or Alex No-Soil Compost early in February in boxes in the greenhouse at a temperature of 55 degrees F. Sow very shallowly and then press the seed with a wooden presser into the firmed compost and sift the merest skittering of silver sand over the top. Give a light watering through the fine rose of a can, cover the box with a sheet of glass and a sheet of brown paper and put on the staging of the greenhouse.

Every day remove the glass at about 9 o'clock in the morning for wiping and put it back immediately. When the seedlings are through, take off the glass and paper completely and allow the plants to grow on slowly. When they are about 1 in. high pot up directly into 3-in. pots containing Alex No-Soil Compost 1 and put these pots on the staging of the greenhouse at a temperature of 50 degrees F.

Potting On

When the roots of the plants in the 3-in. pots are starting to curl round inside, pot the plants on into 5-in. pots using John Innes Potting Compost 2 or Alex No-Soil Compost 2. By early May it should be possible to do the third potting, i.e. into the 9-in. pots in which the plants are to grow and flower. This time use John Innes Compost 3 or Alex No-Soil Compost 3. By about the 20th of the month it should be possible to put the plants outside into a nice sunny spot which is sheltered from high winds.

When the plants are in their 3-in. pots, it is a good thing to pinch out the growing points of the plants, ten days or a fortnight after potting up, to ensure branching. As the result of such pinching branches will grow to 4 or 5 ft in height, and there may easily be a span of the same length from one side of the flowering stems to the other. Of course, if the plants are to be grown in one of the special ways described further on then the methods of stopping and training will be different.

General Culture

The plants have to be regularly watered all the time they are growing because the thousands of leaves transpire a tremendous amount of moisture. It is equally necessary to feed regularly once the plants are 18 in. or so high. Diluted Marinure or Farmura can be given once a week until the flowers open.

The usual precautions have to be taken against pests and diseases. Nicotine may be used to prevent attacks of leaf miner, aphids and capsids. Karathane may be applied to control attacks of mildew.

Six Main Methods of Training

A brief description must be given of the six main ways plants can be trained. For these trained plants it is usual to decide on definite colours and for this purpose stock plants are selected in December according to their colour. These, when they have been cut down early in January, are set aside for cutting production; the cuttings are struck in the normal way as advised in Chapter 3.

The stopping or pinching back that the gardener is advised to carry out should cease about the middle of September. By that time the type of plant to be grown should have been formed. It is during the fourth week in September that the plants are brought in from outside, and placed on the greenhouse staging in a little heat. These Cascade Chrysanthemums will grow quite happily in low temperatures with plenty of ventilation. It is necessary, however, to have sufficient heat to keep out the frost and to keep the atmosphere in the greenhouse buoyant.

1. *The True Cascade*   The plant, at a very early stage, should be reduced to two leading shoots. The pots should then be placed on a shelf or on a wall, preferably facing south and anything from 4 to 4½ ft above ground level. A 6-ft-long bamboo stake should then be securely tied to another bamboo which has been pushed down well into the 9-in. pot as shown in the drawing. The leading shoots will be trained down this bamboo.

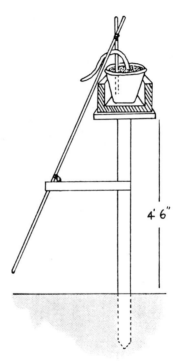

How to start the training of a Cascade Chrysanthemum

All the original shoots should be stopped at two or three leaves, and stopped again as required to make bushy lateral growth – the leader or end growth then being allowed to grow on – and tied to the bamboo stake as growth progresses. Attention should be given to this procedure every few days during the growing season. At the end of September, the stakes should be removed and the pots placed on a shelf or pedestal in the cool greenhouse, by which time the plants will be 4 to 6 ft long. It is advisable, when the plant is in position in the house, to fix the ends of the longest shoots to some support to prevent the plants being damaged.

2. *Standards* When making the final potting it is important that a good strong stake should be firmly planted right to the bottom of the pot, and rising to a height of 3 ft above the rim. The leader is trained on this stake, and in due course it will have to support the head of the plant.

From the beginning the leader should be given freedom of growth, all side shoots being pinched out until a height of about 2 to 3 ft is reached, when the leader is stopped. Two or three side shoots are then allowed to develop, after which the plant will be stopped and re-stopped every two or three leaves, to build up a 'mop'-like head. This building-up process continues until the first or second week in September.

While the plants are being trained outside on the ashes, it is as well to have the supporting stakes tied to a cross wire to prevent the wind blowing the plants over, especially when the head is developing.

3. *Umbrellas* The same method is used here as for the standard, except that a wire frame, shaped like the cover of an umbrella and approximately 3 ft in diameter, is secured to the stake 3 ft above pot level. When the leader reaches the height of $2\frac{1}{2}$ ft, it is stopped and the side shoots developed in the same way as for the standard form, except that in this case they are kept tied down to the wire frame. The whole of the frame should be covered by the time stopping ceases in September.

4. *Weeping Forms* As in the method for the umbrella form, a wire frame is secured to a stake 3 ft above pot level, but the wire frame need only be 12 to 15 in. in diameter. Six to eight pieces of string are then tied from the frame to the top of the pot.

As with the umbrella form, the leader is stopped at about $2\frac{1}{2}$ ft, and then six to eight side shoots are allowed to develop. These are grown up through and over the edge of the frame, and so down the strings, all side growths being stopped until the leaders have reached the top of the pot. When the plant is coming into flower carefully remove the strings.

5. *Pillar or Upright Forms* Another method of training that has been much admired is the pillar or upright form. This is obtained by keeping the plant to one leader and stopping the laterals at every second or third leaf, exactly as for the cascade form, but the leader is allowed to grow upright and is tied to a stout bamboo stake as growth proceeds. It is therefore possible,

by this means, to obtain a tall pillar of colour from 4 to 7 ft high, producing a most unusual decorative effect. The plants should be turned every day or two, otherwise the growth will be one-sided.

6. *Fan-trained Forms*   At the final potting in May, two plants of the same colour (or two different colours if desired) should be potted on side by side in the one pot. When potting, three stout bamboo stakes should also be fixed in the pot, one rising to a height of $4\frac{1}{2}$ ft in the centre, and the other two down the sides of the pot, thus giving as wide an angle at the top as possible. These three stout bamboos are used as the foundation for the thinner horizontal canes, which should be tied on about 6 in. apart, starting about 3 in. above the rim of the pot.

The bottom cane should be at least 4 ft across, and each succeeding cane should be slightly shorter as they rise, so as to make as near as possible a half-circle or fan. The first stopping should be at about 6 in., and from then on it is a matter of stopping at frequent intervals to get as many leaders and side shoots as are necessary to build up the fan and fill in all spaces as the plant grows.

Varieties

There are no true varieties as such. Suttons' Cascade seed, however, produces plants bearing beautiful pink, white, rose, bronze, yellow and orange flowers.

16 Unusual Types: Anemones, Thread-petalled and Pompons

There are a number of unusual chrysanthemums that people like to grow as a curiosity or because they become very fond of them. It isn't every nurseryman that stocks the unusual kinds mentioned in this chapter, and if there are readers who have difficulty in getting the kinds and types they require, I will be only too glad to pass on the names and addresses of nurserymen who can supply their needs.

Anemone

Anemone Chrysanthemums, often called Anemone-centred Chrysanthemums, are becoming very popular for floral decorations. Readers who have travelled to Canada and America will know how popular this particular type of chrysanthemum is there, and how they are divided very definitely into two groups, (a) the Large-flowered and (b) the Medium-flowered. Do not be misled, however, by people who say that the varieties are completely hardy, for although they will live through a normal frost they are invariably killed by persistent frosts, especially when grown in the north of England.

Cultivation
The varieties grow to a height of anything from 4 ft to 5 ft, but lately some nurserymen have been claiming that they stock smaller varieties than this, which they advise should be grown in 5-in. pots (see Chapter 9). The taller kinds that grow in pots should be managed as advised in Chapter 8.

Timing and Stopping
I have found it advisable, in the case of almost all the Anemone-centred varieties I have grown, to make two stoppings, the first about 15 March and the second about 15 June. This is to allow two good shoots to develop after the first stopping and two further shoots after the second stopping, thus making four in all. If then the normal disbudding is carried out some very lovely flowers are produced.

124

*An Anemone-centred
Chrysanthemum*

Out of Doors

It is possible, in the south of England, to grow the plants out of doors in a sunny sheltered bed. Here they should be planted 18 in. apart and in normal years they would be flowering early in November. In very wet seasons, the plants require some protection. Drive posts into the ground and between these stretch a length of strong butter muslin above the plants to give them some protection.

The alternative is to dig the plants up with a good ball of soil to the roots and bring them into the greenhouse as advised in Chapter 7.

Varieties

In most cases the ray florets which grow right round the outside of the flower are of quite a different colour to the disc florets which grow in the centre of the blooms. The name Anemone-centred arises from this. Very interesting contrasts are produced. It is possible, for instance, to have a golden bronze cushion centre with a brick-red surround, or a greeny-blue centre with a deep lilac surround.

Name	*Description*	*Large- or Medium-flowered*
GREENHOUSE VARIETIES		
Admiration	rose-shaded apricot cushion, deep rose petals around	large
American Gain	brick-red with cushion of golden bronze	large
American Success	deep lilac flowers with cream lilac cushion	large
André	deep salmon, yellow centre	large
Basile	lemon with tint of red at centre, green eye	medium-large
Beautiful Lady	delicate pink, creamy cushion	medium
Brigida	deep purple petals, green eye, purple-lilac cushion	medium
Cassino	pale pink cushion, deep rose petals	medium
Conrado	very small cushion, apricot	medium
Edmundo	pure lilac, green centre, spoon	large
Erberto	rose-purple, yellow cushion green eye	large
Ethel Anderson	red, with red cushion	medium
Grace Land	white with yellow cushion	large
Lazare	deep chestnut with light chestnut cushion, green centre	large
Magdalena	golden-yellow centre, spoon	large
Marion Stacey	rich old rose with white cushion	large

Pietro	red petals, yellow cushion green centre	medium
Riccardo	salmon cushion, bright green centre	medium
Susanna	clear white with bright yellow small cushion	medium
Timoteo	light ruby with same coloured cushion	medium
Vivien	red petals, inner circle of golden florets, green centre	medium
Yellow Graceland	yellow	medium

OUTDOOR VARIETIES

Catena	reddish bronze with amber cushion	medium
Mini Minnie	delicate pink with tinted cushion	large
Premier	golden yellow, cushion same colour	medium

Thread-petalled

Thread-petalled Chrysanthemums are sometimes called Spidery Chrysanthemums because the petals are said to look like spider's legs. The plants are grown in exactly the same way as normal Single-flowered Chrysanthemums, as described in Chapter 10. No stopping is done at all, for the plants break naturally. The cuttings are usually struck from 15 February to 5 March in the normal way, and when they are fully rooted they are potted up into 3-in. pots containing Alex No-Soil Compost 1. From these they are usually potted on into 5-in. pots. Use Alex No-Soil Compost 2, making certain that the compost is really firm. With Thread-petalled varieties it pays to under-pot rather than over-pot, and to pot very firmly.

The pot plants are grown out of doors until the beginning of October, when they are brought into the greenhouse at a temperature of about 50 degrees F.

Varieties

Name	Description	Time of Flowering
Bendigo Bronze	golden bronze with golden petal points, spidery	November
Cyrillus	lilac, green centre, spiky, spidery	November–December
Edgarus	long thin spiky fawn petals with spoon-shaped red tops	November–December
Green Nightingale	large, sea-green	November
Martinus	red, delicate spiky florets, green eye, spidery	November–December
Miss Dorothy Tuthill	bronze, spidery	November–December
Mrs Carter	golden yellow	November

A Thread-petalled Chrysanthemum

Rayonnante	mauvy-lilac	November
Sandra Gail	red-bronze, spidery	October–November
Theodorus	light bronze, rolled spiky petals, tinted red at tips	November–December
Tokyo	pure white, spidery	November
White Spider	white, spidery, with strong stems	November
Yellow Rayonnante	largish yellow	November

Pompons

Pompons, sometimes called Pompoms and sometimes Pompomes, may be said to be a 'come-back'. They were very popular in the early Victorian era and when the bigger types were introduced they were gradually neglected. Now they are coming into popularity once more. All the plants are dwarf in habit and growth, and all the flowers are double and round in shape.

The plants are quite hardy and will normally grow well in the open, being similar in this respect to the Koreans. They make very good cut flowers and are useful in the herbaceous border. It is possible to pot up some specimens and bring them into the house for decoration. The October-flowering plants can be grown specially in 5-in. pots for the greenhouse or home.

Cultivation

There is nothing particular to say about the cultivation of Pompons – they will do happily in almost any soil, they can be propagated as advised for Koreans and there is no stopping or disbudding to do at all. They are therefore one of the easiest types of chrysanthemum to grow.

Varieties

All varieties of Pompons are really designed to grow out of doors, but latterly varieties have been introduced which definitely flower in November and so must be grown under glass in most parts of the country.

Name	Description	Height
GARDEN POMPON VARIETIES		
Anastasia	rich wine on thin stems	2 ft
Apricot Roach	delicate apricot	18 in.
Audrey Godfrey	pink, salmon centre	2 ft
Babyface	pink, dark centre	2 ft
Bronze Fairie	bronze, sport of Fairie	12 in.
Bunty	white, bronze centre	18 in.
Cameo	white	15 in.
Cathie	pink	18 in.
Cathie	deep pink	30 in.

Cascade and Charm Chrysanthemums

Dave Miles	pink, salmon centre	18 in.
Denise	golden flowers	12 in.
Dresden China	pink lavender, flushed gold	15 in.
Dusky	blood-red	12 in.
Ethel	bright red	15 in.
Eve	purple, medium flowers	2 ft
Fairie	pink	12 in.
Flora	light lilac	18 in.
Fred Raynor	cream	2 ft
Gold Tit	gold, red centre	18 in.
Heiress	yellow, red eye	12 in.
Jante Wells	golden yellow	15 in.
Kiki	pale pink, good spray for decoration	2 ft
Kip Miles	Apricot, one of the earliest poms	18 in.
Ladybird	chestnut-bronze, neat compact plants	18 in.
Lilac Roach	lilac tinted, salmon centre	18 in.
Liz Raynor	shell-pink to salmon	2 ft
Lottie	bright red with bronzy tint	2 ft
Mitzie	creamy-white, green centre	18 in.
Mosquito	intense yellow	18 in.
Nell Raynor	two-tone shades of salmon	18 in.
Orange Roach	deep orange	15 in.
Pearl Roach	pearl to salmon centre	2 ft
Peggy Clarke	lilac pink, shading to salmon	18 in.
Pink Puff	pink with yellowish green centre	15 in.
Pink Roach	delicate light pink pom, good habit	18 in.
Salmon Fairie	rich salmon sport from Fairie	15 in.
Sam Miles	light salmon with deeper centre	2 ft
Sarah Roach	deep autumn rose	18 in.
Solley	gold with orange centre	12 in.
Sunset	true flaming bronze to orange	18 in.
Tiara	bronze compact flowers	18 in.
Tommy Trout	amber at the edges, bronze centre	18 in.
Waltz Maris	delicate primrose	18 in.
White Bouquet	pure white	2 ft
Yellow Bouquet	glowing yellow	18 in.
Yellow Dot	bright yellow	18 in.
Zena's Roach	salmon to apricot	15 in.

Pink Long Island Beauty, an Anemone-centred Chrysanthemum

17 Pests and Diseases

When it comes to pests and diseases the gardening author faces two big problems. First of all he doesn't want to frighten the would-be chrysanthemum grower by giving a long list of troubles that must be faced. Secondly, there is very little doubt that the moment the book has been published more information will become available on the control of some particular trouble. All he can do, therefore, is to make the book as up-to-date as possible.

Pests and diseases seem to be on the increase instead of on the decrease. This is not only because our exchange of plants and varieties is now international. Pests now come in in the fuselages of aeroplanes, whereas in the past they took far longer to arrive from the east or the west, in liners and tramp steamers.

There is also the problem of the non-gardeners. There are far too many so-called gardens in towns and suburbia that are not cultivated at all, and there diseases and pests breed happily. How often the author has discovered a keen gardener with his beautiful garden situated between the land of two men who never do a hand's turn on the soil. Modern gardeners, however, have great advantages over those who had to do similar work fifty years ago. There are new insecticides and fungicides, and also biologists have studied the life histories of most of our garden troubles today and have told us when to spray and what to spray with.

I am told that the Chinese pay their doctors weekly when they are well, and cease to pay them immediately they are ill. The doctors in that country, therefore, concentrate definitely on health. The gardener must take his message from China because there is no doubt that plants are less readily attacked by pests and diseases if they are growing happily in good soil fed in the right way.

If you take care of the soil in which the plants grow, the chrysanthemum plants will be really sturdy and will resist the troubles to which weak plants are prone. Feed carefully as directed, water when necessary and never allow the plants to be coddled. See, too, that they have all the light they need.

Recognition

Many amateurs fail to achieve good control with insecticides or fungicides because they are never able to diagnose the trouble correctly. It is useless to try and kill the insect that sucks the sap from *inside* a leaf with a poison that is deposited on the top of a leaf. It is foolish to apply Captan, an excellent fungicide, in the hope of controlling aphids. Invest in a good magnifying glass, examine the parts of the plants carefully, and so be able to be quite sure whether the trouble is due to insect attack or an inroad of fungi.

Learn to apply the right remedy at the right time and in the correct manner. There is usually one most vulnerable stage in the life history of any enemy and if the cure can only be applied then the victory is won. To dust or spray long before or long after the critical period may be absolutely useless.

Fungus Diseases

I always describe the fungus as a lowly plant living and growing on another plant. It produces its little branches and it is these that the gardener sees with the naked eye as a spot or a powdery mass. Minute branches produce little sacks of seed (or spores as they are called) and when blown about by the wind they land on the leaves and stems of other plants. There they germinate and send their little roots into the plant tissue. The Mycelium, as the roots should be called, then work their way through the root or stem tissue and eventually send up other little branches with many more sacks of spores and thus the fungus disease spreads day after day.

The gardener who wants to prevent a bad attack of a disease, such as mildew or rust, must cover the leaves or stems with a protective layer of a fungicide. When the baby spore drops on to the surface of any part of the plant it will immediately be killed before it has a chance of sending down its roots into the tissue. There are four main types of fungicides. The first, based on sulphur, is applied as sulphur dust, lime sulphur, colloidal sulphur and liver of sulphur. The sulphur dusts are usually prepared with a kaolin carrier where the particles are very fine and so completely cover each leaf.

The disadvantage of using some of the sulphur preparations is that they do not mix happily with any of the petroleum oil preparations.

The second type is based on copper and is used as Bordeaux, copper-lime dust or colloidal copper. Colloidal copper can be mixed with petroleum oil preparations and doesn't leave an unpleasant stain on the leaves. Colloidal coppers are diluted with water in accordance with the instructions on the container.

The third is Captan, which can be applied as a dust or as a spray. It is non-poisonous to human beings and animals but injurious to fish in pools. It is excellent in controlling and preventing the damping-off trouble of chrysanthemum blooms and is much used for rusts also. Orthocide Captan is most effective for many garden diseases but must not be allowed to contaminate feeding stuffs.

The fourth is Karathane, which is extremely good for preventing the powdery mildew on the leaves of chrysanthemums. Apply the powder by spray before the disease appears and repeat the dose at ten-day intervals as and when necessary. Some chrysanthemum growers have told me that Karathane has caused a little trouble on one or two varieties, but I have not experienced this.

Mr Jack Woolman recommends Combinex as an excellent spray against mildew. It is also an insecticide of reasonable value.

The Main Fungus Diseases

Aspermy

This, theoretically, is a virus disease, but I am including it here for the sake of convenience. This particular disease is giving a lot of trouble all over the world. It causes flower distortion and yet doesn't seem to damage the leaves at all. It may cause the florets to twist or look ragged or become tubular. The virus is carried by aphids, usually during the propagating period, and that is the time to spray with Malathion, a systemic* insecticide which will ensure that all the aphids are killed.

Control Watch plants carefully and never save those which produce distorted flowers. Cuttings must only be taken from perfectly healthy specimens.

Never allow aphids to visit chrysanthemums, especially in the cutting stage. Spray with strong liquid derris.

Botrytis

This is sometimes called mould disease and is caused by the fungus *Botrytis chrysanthemi*. The blooms become covered with a

* An insecticide which penetrates right through the system.

greyish fluffy powder which first occurs on the undersides of the petals and then all over the flowers. It may later appear on the stems and leaves. It gives a lot of trouble when the plants are overcrowded and is very bad in cold houses where the conditions are humid. It spreads because of the white spores which float in the air.

Control Never give chrysanthemums too much nitrogen because it is when they grow soft that the plants are more susceptible to attack. Keep the air in the greenhouse as dry as possible because then the fungus will shrivel. Provide adequate ventilation in the greenhouse and maintain a buoyant atmosphere.

Use Captan as a dust, applying it as a mist all over the plants when the blooms first show colour.

Never allow infected blooms to stay in the greenhouse, for they are the means whereby the disease will spread.

Leaf Spot
This disease is caused by the fungus *Septoria chrysanthemi*. Dark brown patches appear on the upper surfaces of the lower leaves in summer. Actually, they first start as yellowy green patches which then go brown and finally black. In bad cases the entire leaf will succumb. The disease works its way upwards and I have seen plants where this disease has killed nearly all the foliage.

Control Always burn severely attacked plants to prevent the trouble from spreading. The fungus undoubtedly lives on any leaves left in the garden in the winter.

Spray with Bordeaux mixture with a colloidal copper wash the moment the trouble is first seen. Remember that the disease always attacks the lower leaves first, so see that the nozzle of the spraying machine is directed to cover the upper and lower surfaces of the foliage at the base of the plant. Mr Jack Woolman recommends Zineb.

Mildew
White powdery patches are seen not only on the leaves but on the stems as well. This white growth, which is the fungus *Oidium chrysanthemi*, appears towards the end of the season and starts on the under surface of the leaves. These eventually turn a brownish colour and then drop off. It may occur out of doors on plants grown on dry soil and it is important, therefore, to flood

the ground where chrysanthemums are growing in droughty weather.

In the greenhouse the trouble is encouraged by high humidity and it always pays to heat the house a little so as to provide a buoyant atmosphere.

Control   It is important to control this powdery white fungus in the early stages because severe attacks can cause leaf distortion and the death of the bulk of the foliage.

Karathane is the ideal fungicide for this disease. Out of doors it can be applied as a powder from puffer packs, and under glass Karathane can be used as a smoke because then the fungicide is evenly distributed all over the area. Karathane smokes are lit in the evening when the house is closed down, and early in the morning the door and ventilator should be opened to let out the excess fumes.

Rust

This is a particularly bad disease in some years. Red rusty spots like minute cushions are usually seen first on the under surfaces of the leaves and they may be in ring formation. On the upper surfaces of the same leaves light circular yellow dots appear which correspond with pustules found below. As the disease progresses the leaves may turn brown and drop off. Sometimes the leaf dries up and hangs on to the stem.

The trouble is caused by a fungus *Puccinia chrysanthemi*. The spores may be carried by wind or by splashed water, rain drops or dew.

Control   Spray with a thiram wash the moment the trouble is seen, dissolving 2 oz of thiram in 3 gallons of water. It may even be advisable to spray before the rust is discerned in gardens where the disease is serious year after year.

Never give overdoses of nitrogen to chrysanthemums because the leaves will then soften and rust can more easily attack. Be careful also never to over-water because this seems to predispose the plants to rust disease.

Virus

One of the viruses has been dealt with under the heading Aspermy. Viruses cannot be thought of as true diseases but they are included under this heading because they are not insect pests. Perhaps the worst virus at the present time is Spotted

Wilt. The first thing the gardener sees, as a rule, is a couple of yellow rings on the leaves followed by light green spots on the youngest leaves and maybe bronze spots and rings on the old leaves. Later the leaves may twist and curl downwards and the whole of the plant looks peculiarly stunted.

Though most viruses are spread by aphids, Spotted Wilt is undoubtedly spread by thrips in the larval stage.

Control   There is no control of Spotted Wilt. It is important to burn badly affected plants and equally important to keep down thrips.

Verticilium Wilt

The lower leaves pale and wilt, particularly at the margin at first. Later the whole leaf is affected, wilts completely and dies. Sometimes the trouble seems to keep to the lower leaves and at other times it rises right up the plant; often only one side of the plant is affected at the beginning. The symptons are seldom seen until the flower buds appear.

Control   Never propagate from Verticilium-infected plants. Propagate by cuttings as late as possible so that they are really long and vigorous. The tips of these vigorous shoots make good cuttings, free from disease. Avoid growing susceptible varieties.

Insect Pests

It was my old friend, the late Mr G. Fox Wilson, the Entomologist of the Royal Horticultural Society, who did a tremendous amount of work on the pests of chrysanthemums. I saw him year after year at Wisley and at the RHS Shows.

It is possible to divide insect pests arbitrarily into two main classes: those that suck, like aphids and capsid bugs, and those that nibble and eat, like the defoliating caterpillars. In addition, however, there are others which tunnel in the leaves like the leaf miner or, like the Frosted Orange Moth, which burrow into the stem. Fortunately the latter is rare.

The grower must be on his guard because there are over eighty distinct species of insect pests that will attack chrysanthemums. I have not, however, included every possible pest but only those that are commonly met with in gardens and greenhouses today.

The gardener must examine his plants carefully, starting with the buds and then go on to the foliage. Damaged buds may go blind and this trouble may be due to earwigs or capsids. The foliage may be attacked by aphids that suck underneath the leaves, eelworms that tunnel inside, and caterpillars which consume both leaves and stem. If little galls are seen, then the Chrysanthemum Gall Midge must be suspected, while if the leaves are mottled, the trouble may be due to the Leaf Hopper, the Red Spider or the White Fly.

Flowers may be distorted by thrips or malformed by capsids. They may be eaten away by cockroaches, earwigs or caterpillars. With regard to shoots and stems, these may be distorted by frog-hoppers, eaten away by millipedes or by one of the caterpillars. Tunnelling at the bottom of the stem may be done by wireworms.

Even the roots may be attacked, by root aphis, leather-jackets, millipedes or vine weevils. There is a Stool Mining Maggot which occasionally gives trouble. If when the plant is dug up largish galls are found on the roots, then undoubtedly the trouble is due to the Root Knot Eelworm.

The Main Insect Pests

Aphids

Amateurs refer to aphids as greenflies, blackflies and so on. These breed very quickly indeed, especially in the spring and summer. They feed by sucking the sap, and distort the shoots, tear the leaves and even malform the flowers. They are the carriers of the Aspermy virus and maybe other viruses too. If they are not checked on the plants outside they may easily be carried into the greenhouse on the leaves and then they go on producing their young throughout the winter months.

Control Spray regularly with a good liquid derris. Once the plants are in the greenhouse it is possible to fumigate by using modern smokes.

Capsid Bugs

There are three capsid bugs which may attack chrysanthemums from about the middle of July to the middle of October. These are the Tarnished Plant Bug, the Bishop Bug and the Potato Capsid (*Lygus pabulimus, Lygus pritensis* and *Lygus leucorum*).

If the capsids are brought into the greenhouses on the plants at the end of October they may easily continue to give trouble throughout the winter months. Outside these capsids will shelter among rubbish, under hedges and in cracks of the fencing, so that they can become a nuisance again in the spring. They feed by sucking, pushing their needle-like proboscis into the leaf buds or shoots and so stunting them. They can pucker the leaves and cause malformed shoots. They quickly drop to the ground when the gardener approaches a plant and even his shadow will disturb them.

Control   Collect all the debris that drops under the hedgerows. Spray gooseberry bushes (as this is the alternative host) in February with Dinitro-Ortho-Cresol in order to kill the eggs of this pest. Spray the plants with a pyrethrum extract, giving them a thorough soaking, early in July and once every three weeks until the middle of September. Be sure to spray the ground around the plants on to which the capsid bugs may have fallen.

Caterpillars
There are a number of different kinds of caterpillar which will eat the leaves of chrysanthemums. Some caterpillars do most damage during the night.

Control   Spray immediately the trouble is seen with an efficient derris or pyrethrum wash. Under glass burn one of the smokes in the evening after the house has been closed down. The greenhouse must be opened up early in the morning.

Chrysanthemum Midge
This is a pest which was introduced from the USA. The eggs are laid on young shoots with the result that galls are seen like small thorns. One female can lay 150 eggs. The midges will attack the stems and buds with the result that the flowers are crippled and distorted. Eggs can hatch out every five or six days and so the generations quickly overlap one another.

Control   This is by no means a common pest and when it is seen it pays to burn the affected plants immediately. Spraying with derris plus pyrethrum twice a week for six weeks will keep the trouble down in the case of slight attacks.

Cuckoo Spit
This is sometimes known as the Frog Hopper, its Latin name being *Philaenus spunarius*. Most people know the spittle-like appearance of this pest. It produces this spittle, of course, to prevent its being eaten by birds. It sucks the sap of the plants, usually attacking the undersides of the leaves, and may cause

these to curl up. It is generally found first in the middle of June. Later on in the season it becomes quite a large brown insect $\frac{1}{4}$ in. long, and it jumps. At this stage it punctures the stalk under the flower bud, perhaps causing it to bend over, and sucks the sap. It may also puncture the flower bud and suck the sap.

Control   Spray with pyrethrum extract the moment the trouble is seen.

Earwigs
Earwigs are too well known to need description. They often attack half-opened flowers and they damage the growing points of plants.

Control   Fill 3-in. flower pots with straw or hay and put them upside down on bamboos among the chrysanthemums. The earwigs go in there early in the morning and hide, and then the gardener may easily knock them out into a little can of paraffin.

Some growers have had success by putting a $\frac{1}{2}$-in.-wide band of Vaseline on the stems of the plants a couple of inches or so below the blooms.

Dusting around the base of the stems of plants with a strong derris-pyrethrum dust will kill the pests, but it is apt to kill the predators also. (Predators are insects which feed on other insects.)

Eelworm
The eelworm may be considered the most important pest of chrysanthemums. They cannot be seen with the naked eye for they are translucent and only 1 mm long. The chrysanthemum eelworm moves up the plant on the outside of the stem in films of moisture. When it reaches a leaf it enters through the small pores and then wriggles in between the leaf cells in the air spaces. There it starts to feed with the result that the cells turn brown. It is this browning which tells the gardener that eelworm is present.

As it only takes ten days for adults to lay eggs and for the larvae which hatch out to develop into adults, it is clear that a big population can build up inside a leaf, especially as every female can lay thirty eggs. Experts have found as many as 10,000 eelworms in one chrysanthemum leaf. The lower leaves are infested first and gradually the eelworms climb up the plant, getting into the leaves higher up.

Eelworms can move from plant to plant in the soil as well as over the weeds between plants. Not only will the leaves turn brown when infested but also they may be distorted. Later the eelworm may attack the flower bud, making this brown and distorted as well.

Control   To eliminate eelworm it is necessary to immerse the stools of the plants in water at exactly 115 degrees F for five minutes. Care must be taken not to raise the temperature above 115 degrees F nor to exceed the period of five minutes. This treatment kills the eelworms in the early stages.

It is good to know that the eelworm does not persist in the soil throughout the winter if the ground is kept perfectly free from weeds.

Leaf Miner

The little maggots which tunnel tortuously in the leaves hatch out from eggs laid by a brown fly similar to a house fly but half the size. The female of this fly lays her eggs between the upper and lower skins of the leaves. The maggot which hatches out and does the tunnelling is about $\frac{1}{8}$ in. long. When this maggot has fully grown it pupates and it is possible to see the yellowy brown pupa sticking out slightly from one of the tunnels on the under side of the leaf. A new fly will emerge later from the pupa. This will lay more eggs and so continue to cause trouble.

Control   Spray the plants with nicotine or, under glass, burn Auto-Shreds at night-time. Repeat the dose in a fortnight's time and again a fortnight after that if necessary.

Leather-Jacket

This, of course, is the larvae of the Daddy Longlegs or Crane Fly. The larvae live for one season in this form and they attack the chrysanthemum stems just about soil level. I have known young plants to be severed from the roots. In the older plants a ring may be eaten right around the stems. This greyish-brown grub which may be up to $1\frac{1}{2}$ in. long when fully grown is called, in the north, 'the Bot'. It is quite legless and has a leathery skin, hence its name. In my garden the trouble usually starts in September with the roots being nibbled.

Control   It is not difficult to find the grubs in the day-time hidden in the soil just below the plants. When found they can be picked up and dropped into a little tin of paraffin.

Slugs

There are many different types of slug but the ones that usually attack chrysanthemums are known as 'the small grey'. The greatest damage is done to the shoots that rise from the stools in the winter in frames or cold houses.

Control   Before plunging the stools into the sedge peat or compost, it may be necessary to wash them completely clear of soil and thus of the slug eggs as well.

Where this has not been done, it is necessary to use Draza blue pellets in among the stools; slugs will go for these instead of the chrysanthemum shoots and will be killed.

Stool-Miner

The trouble is caused by a small two-winged fly which appears in April or early May and lays its eggs in the soil near the chrysanthemum plants. Yellowish white larvae looking like small wire-worms hatch out and can be distinguished from the former in that their bodies taper at both ends.

These larvae tunnel into the roots and underground stems and deep wounds may appear. The greatest amount of trouble is done in the autumn in the stool beds.

Control   Get hold of tablets of mercuric chloride. Dissolve these at the rate of $\frac{1}{4}$oz in a $2\frac{1}{2}$-gallon bucket of water. Use this to water well around the stools.

Thrips

These are tiny little black insects which can hardly be seen with the naked eye. They are minute and narrow-bodied. They can be discovered by tapping a plant over a clean white handkerchief; the thrips will show up as little black specks, almost like a streak of soot. When fully grown the thrips are $\frac{1}{16}$ in. long and people with good eyesight can see them on the petals of white blooms.

Thrips usually attack the flowers and especially so in a droughty period. The creatures will hide in the centre of the blooms when they are disturbed or frightened. I have found them on sunny days on the underside of chrysanthemum leaves.

Control   Spray the plants with a pyrethrum or nicotine wash, preferably on a nice sunny day. Be sure to soak the undersides of the leaves and the growing points of the plants. Give another spraying on the next dry day a week or two later.

White Fly

The White Fly will attack all sorts of greenhouse plants and when one taps the plants the flies may rise like a cloud. The nymphs are like scales attached to the undersides of the leaves. They give out a certain amount of 'honeydew' with the result that sooty-mould, which lives on this substance, may appear and cause the undersides of the foliage to look black.

Control This trouble is only serious in the greenhouse and can be controlled with one of the insecticidal smoke bombs obtainable from any good horticultural chemist. These bombs give out their fumes when lit at night, and must be used in accordance with the cubic capacity of the greenhouse. Be sure to open up the greenhouse early in the morning after fumigation.

Wireworms

Wireworms are the larvae of the Click Beetle. This beetle may be seen flying about in the sun during the months of May and June. After the females have laid their eggs the larvae hatch out after a month and feed first of all on grass, as a rule. They then go on growing and feeding in the soil for four or five years before turning into beetles again.

Wireworms have only three pairs of short legs situated on the first three segments of their bodies. This makes it easy to distinguish them from centipedes. Also, wireworms are as tough as their name suggests, orangey-brown in colour and from 1 to $1\frac{1}{4}$ in. in length.

They tunnel up the roots of chrysanthemums and attack the stems. I have found wireworms a good 6 in. up the stem of a plant.

Control If the ground is known to be infected with wireworms, dress the ground with wireworm dust at the rate of $\frac{1}{2}$oz to 1 sq. yd three weeks before planting out. Rake this in thoroughly.

In cases where wireworms were not known to be present until after planting, dust a wireworm dust among the plants at 2 oz to 1 sq. yd and rake in shallowly. Give a second dusting three weeks later with the same quantity.

Woodlice

Woodlice, sometimes called peabugs, monkey bugs or slaters may damage the young shoots as they grow up from the stools of plants.

Control   Do everything possible to get rid of the spots where the woodlice may breed: rough edging stone to a path, for instance, the debris under hedges, old rubbish dumps and the like. Dust with derris-pyrethrum all around the hiding places of these insect pests and when the damage is actually seen use derris dust on the soil among the plants in the frames and greenhouse.

Glossary of Terms Used in Chrysanthemum Growing

Gardeners have a habit of using a jargon of their own. Therefore, in order that any particular words used in the book may be fully understood, I am including this glossary, plus a certain number of explanatory diagrams. As I have said in my preface, it may be quite a good idea for readers who are new to chrysanthemum growing to read the glossary first.

Anticipated natural break
If the gardener is dealing with a variety that produces an abundance of shoots early on, he usually pinches out the tip of the plant before the break bud is seen, and thus anticipates what is going to happen naturally. Hence the term used above. As a result, flowers will be produced which are called the first 'crown' buds.

Axil of leaf
The axil of a leaf is the angle between the upper side of the leaf and the stem. In the axil of a leaf may be found buds or little laterals.

Break
A side growth, sometimes called a lateral growth. When the term 'to break' is used, it refers to the sending out of a side growth or branch.

Compost
A confusing term sometimes used to indicate the rotting down of vegetable refuse or straw for producing an excellent substitute for farmyard manure. It is also used to describe a mixture of soil, peat and sand, or sand and peat alone, prepared for the striking of cuttings or the growing of chrysanthemums in pots. There are two main potting composts used today, one called John Innes, the other Alex No-Soil.

143

Crown bud

The first crown bud is the first bud found at the end of a branch produced on the main stem of a plant. It is called a natural first crown when it is produced naturally. When the tip of the main stem is pinched out before the break bud has formed, it is of course an artificial first crown. The bud of the first crown, incidentally, invariably produces the largest flower although not necessarily the best bloom.

The second crown is the bud produced on the ends of the side growths which grow on the first laterals. Side growths, in fact, have resulted either from the natural production of the first flower bud or from the pinching out of the growing point, which is known as 'stopping'.

Very occasionally late varieties are stopped three times in order to produce a very late crop of flowers. The second crowns are removed and a further batch of laterals are produced, giving third crown flowers which are not usually of good quality.

Cutting

A short growth cut off from the sides of stems of the stools which are unrooted but leafy. Cuttings may also come from the old roots and in both cases they are dibbled into compost where it is hoped they will produce roots.

A cutting is said to have struck when it has produced roots.

Fillis

A special string used by gardeners for tying up chrysanthemums. There is 2-ply, 3-ply and even 4-ply Fillis.

Floret

See *Ray floret and disc floret*.

Hardening off

When plants have been nice and warm, growing in a greenhouse, it is a mistake to put them straight out from this temperature into the cold ground and into a spot where they will have to put up with the normal outside weather. Therefore a gardener takes the plants out of the greenhouse and puts them into a frame or under cloches, where there is some protection but a good deal more air. Gradually he removes the glass protection in the day-time until the plants are hard and can go out into the open.

Lifting
Digging up plants with a ball of soil to the roots, usually in late September or early October, and transferring them into the earth in the greenhouse. It really means planting almost fully grown plants.

Natural break
When a plant is allowed to grow naturally it produces what is known as a 'break bud'. This is a small flower bud which grows at the tip of the main stem, and as a result of its production the plant is checked and a number of branches are produced. Therefore, to allow a plant to break naturally, as it is called, means that you allow it to produce its branches when it will, without adopting any artificial method of inducing side growths to develop.

Node
This means a joint in a stem. It is the part of the stem that normally bears a leaf, or leaves. There is usually a little swelling at that point. The area of stem in between two nodes is known as the inter node.

pH
Scientists have agreed to express the degree of acidity of soil by what seems a queer notation, i.e. pH7. This represents the neutral point; figures less than 7 indicate the degree of acidity, and figures more than 7 show the degree of alkalinity. So a soil that is pH4 is far more acid than a soil that is pH6.

Pinching
This term is used by gardeners to indicate that they are pinching out the growing point of a plant so that the shoots in the axils of the leaves grow out. They do this before the break bud develops naturally, and they do it to ensure that branches will develop much earlier. The word 'timing' was introduced because by pinching off the growing point of a young plant you can make it flower earlier, before its natural time. This is important for commercial growers, who like to get their blooms in early for market. It is important too for gardeners who exhibit and want to have the flowers ready for a certain Show, and also for northerners who want to produce blooms outside before there is a bad frost.

Ray floret and disc floret

In Single Chrysanthemums the florets are of two kinds. There are disc florets in the centre, forming what is normally called the eye, and ray florets around the outside which most amateurs just call 'petals'. Ray florets are really, of course, little flowers on their own. They contain stigma rather like two prongs of a fork, and it is on to this that the pollen lands. It then fertilizes the ovary, which is at the base of the ray floret, and a seed or seeds are produced.

In the disc floret there are stamens which produce the pollen, and this is normally carried by insect visitors to the stigmas. Generally speaking, the stamens do not ripen simultaneously with the stigma in the same floret, and so self-fertilization is very unlikely indeed. Very occasionally the forked stigmas bend back so far that they actually touch the pollen grains, and then of course self-fertilization does take place.

Seedlings

New varieties are described as 'seedlings' when they have actually been raised from seed by specialists who transfer the pollen from one variety to the stigmas of another by hand. They remove any disc florets there are first, to make certain that no self-pollination can take place. Their problem often is that it is very difficult to get male pollen from double varieties, because this is only produced by the disc floret, and in a double variety disc florets may be absent or there may be very few of them.

Standing ground

When chrysanthemums are grown in pots it is necessary to stand these in the open during the summer and then bring them into the greenhouse about the end of September – sometimes a little earlier in the north, and maybe a little later in the south.

In order to prevent the roots of the chrysanthemum growing out of the pots into the ground on which they are standing, and to prevent worms from working their way up into the pots through the drainage hole, the soil is covered with coal ashes to a depth of 3 or 4 in. There should be a fair amount of drainage underneath, and also there should be posts and wires to which the bamboos supporting the chrysanthemums can be tied. This prevents the pots blowing over.

Stool

It will be as well to start with the plant as it is in the autumn or winter, after the blooms have been cut, for then you have the root part of the plant and above it a fairly thick stem, which by then will be quite hard and perhaps only 6 in. long. This clump, with its short old stem, is known as the stool.

Stopping
See *Pinching*.

Sucker
Having dug up the stool, taken off some of the soil, and brought it into the greenhouse, you will expect to find growths, known as suckers, starting to develop from the roots of the stool. These suckers, which are usually rooted, may be detached from the stools and be dibbled out in boxes or frames, but they do not necessarily make good plants.

Terminal bud
The end bud of a branch, usually surrounded by other small buds.

Timing
See *Pinching*.

Appendix

Societies

All readers should join:

1. The Good Gardeners' Association,
   Arkley Manor,
   Arkley,
   Nr Barnet,
   South Herts.

2. The National Chrysanthemum Society
   write to:
   The Secretary,
   Mr S. G. Gosling,
   65 St Margaret's Avenue,
   Whetstone,
   London N20

Chrysanthemum Nurserymen

For chrysanthemum plants of all types and kinds mentioned in this book, by post:

H. Woolman (Dorridge) Ltd,
Grange Road,
Dorridge,
Solihull,
W. Midlands B93 8QB

For Cascade Chrysanthemums from seed:

Sutton & Sons Ltd,
Reading,
Berkshire.

For Korean Chrysanthemums:

The Orpington Nurseries Ltd,
174 Crofton Lane,
Orpington,
Kent.

Index

149

Varieties
–Anemone-centred   18, 124–6, **125**
–Charms   90–1
–Dwarf   24, 84–92
–Korean   84, 86–8, 115–9, **89, 113, 116**
–Large 'Japs'   96–8, **98**
–Mini-mums   84, 91
–Perpetuals   91–2
–Pompoms   24, 88–9, 128–9, **89**
–Single-flowered   93–5, **93**
–Spider-flowered   18, 126, **127**
–Thread-petalled   126–8, **127**

Ventilation of plants   56, 73, 74
   (*see also in chapters on specific types*)
Verticilium Wilt   135

Watering   19, 61–2, 80
–cuttings   58
–syringing   58, 62
Weather   47, 94
Weeding   80
'Weldmesh' wires   61
White fly   141
Wireworms   141
Woodlice   141–2
'Woolmans' Organic Fertilizer'   42